In Love by Accident

" OUCH "

by Dennis F. King

To my friend Mona

Dennis F. King

In Love by Accident

The first meeting

It was a casual encounter, in the aisle, at the grocery store. I shop there once or twice a week to keep my independence. Recently my health took a turn in the wrong direction so here I am, needing help getting around . One thing about life is that nothing stays the same. My mother always said to " Keep your chin up Etta, you are tough like the grandmother you were named after." I am trying to drive my little scooter the store provides but honestly I am not that good at it. The thing jumps ahead as I give it the power, using my thumb, no wonder I am struggling.

The corner was easy enough to turn but as I tried to go straight, my rear tire ran over his foot. The poor guy said " OUCH ". I was so embarrassed and must be apologetic to this man who purposely stood back to give me room to pass. That did not matter at this point since I ran him over anyway.

I turned to speak to him but he was moving towards me in a friendly way. I felt his light hand on my shoulder as he came around to be in front of me. I sheepishly looked up into his face thinking I could bat my eyes too, if it will help.

He was smiling and looking into my eyes and I watched as he looked at my hair, I am so happy I had it done just this morning. When he looked at my lips as I smiled at him I wanted to hide the slight feeling of excitement I had, as a soft shiver went through me. I have not felt like that in a lifetime of looking at men.

I extended my hand to him and said " My name is Etta and I am so, so sorry for hitting you ! " I was looking up into his face but I was very aware of his body right in front of me. He was broad shouldered with a flat stomach, shirt tucked in and very neatly buttoned up except for the top one.

I was attracted to him like two magnets drawn towards each other. Here I am a not so young anymore woman, although my body aches from my new condition. The medication helps me get out of bed to do a few things, like out and about today.

This morning I visited my hairdresser, Edie, my trusted friend and now I have run over a guy's foot. I want to make it up to him because I saw he had tried to stand straight up, back against the canned goods. I hit him anyway and made me wonder if I should be doing this anymore. It is not easy to shop alone when handicapped.

My daughter helps me as much as she can but she has a busy family to care for. I ask her for as little as I can but I do go without things I would like to have.

It is a humbling experience when it sinks in that those days are over of high heels and running upstairs. I gave all my nice shoes away to the homeless charity store.

" My name is Ray and you did not really hurt me ". I was in awe of his soft but deep voice. He spoke slowly but moved quickly as he caught my bouquet of flowers I was treating myself to. He tucked them into my little basket and then asked " Are those from your boyfriend ? " with a smile on his face. I felt so at ease with him. A thought raced through my mind that this is what chemistry is ?

My mind was so flustered that I forgot that I was blocking the aisle too. He stepped back against the shelf and I moved carefully forward. There were three ladies all in a hurry going around us. One lady just shook her head slightly as if to say " move it granny ". The man was older and just walked by us, cane in hand. It became obvious that he was following his busy helper as she stopped to wait for him to catch up to her. Poor guy was trying hard but it did not matter. She was rushing him to get it done.

The last woman was young and well dressed. I could smell her perfume and admired her makeup, it was perfect like her whole outfit. I thought it must be nice to be twenty something and just walking, looks good. The girl has the world at her fingertips. I glanced back up at Ray and to my surprise his eyes were studying me. I was wearing my favorite outfit, shoes and I do my best to look beautiful, every day.

I asked him if he had time for an " I am so sorry, coffee ? " He replied to me " You captured my attention when you ran over my big toe and I like how you are dressed. You speak in such a kind way. I was in here all alone, torn over what I can eat this week. It is always a boring trip to the store before today but I have met a special lady by accident. I would like that very much. Let me walk around the store with you as we both shop to make it a fun experience."

I said " sure, you hold on to the edge of this buggy and we will get through the whole place ". He shook his head in agreement and we proceeded to get everything on our lists. It was so nice to have an interesting and interested friend to shop with. We both favored the vegetable section, that is a good start.

If a woman is smart, she can look in a man's shopping cart to see what goes into him. Remember the saying " you are what you eat ? ". He is carrying around a little basket with paper plates, cookies and some soda with an orange can. I am going to not judge this book by the cover. My mother said " a girl can date anyone she wants to but after forty date who notices you.

The urge in me to have a man friend, boy friend, companion or just a nice guy that understands me, is real. I ask for nothing of anyone but give of myself generously. I deserve happiness even if I have this illness. We never know what can hit us out of the blue sky or our best friend. Our lives are a different story compared to others but a common thread runs through

them all. It is family, friends, love, hurt, pain and happiness. The best way to live is to grab everything you touch with a purpose. You are the writer of your own book.

I wanted to ask him if we could meet later somehow to have a lunch and talk more. He and I both spoke about things we each seemed to enjoy. I wanted more but knew deep in me that I was just a lady in her handicapped cart. I sighed, but did not cry, with that realization.

Just then he said " If you do not mind, I would like to help you put these things away at your home and maybe we can make ourselves a nice lunch ? " The word " yes " came out of my mouth before I could doubt myself. He helped me cash out and loaded my things into my little car as well as holding my door open for me. I said " follow me " and he did.

The ride to my place was tricky for a newcomer because the road has a hairpin turn and then straight up to the top of the only hill in town. We both parked out front and shut off the cars. I was so happy to have a new person around. Ray looked at my little house and then to the left at the big house. The wrought iron fence had recent glossy black paint which gave of a shine like a clean dish will. The building itself was all white with yellow shutters all freshly painted too. He turned to me and noted " they both look the same but one is a doll house." He smiled and looked back and forth while shaking his head " what a view ".

We had a wonderful afternoon talking about a million things. I am too curious by nature and he just answered all my questions. I did it slowly, in between other sentences. It seems he is divorced and has three grown sons. The ex-wife was " burnt out ", in his words, so he was given custody of his children when all three were under ten years old. I was mesmerized by this story coming out of him. How many men could take over a family alone ?

He said " It was my love for them that drove me and I sleep

peacefully at night ". This little conversation let me understand that he has strength and is deeply caring. I was not surprised when he mentioned that he served in the Army and was honorably discharged. I noticed he sat more erect as he mentioned how the military is good for certain people and that not everyone can handle the rigors of it. " I guess I am in that top one percent in America. I am a veteran."

Now I am on my bed about to go to sleep and I can not forget him. What has happened to me ? I feel so relaxed and at peace. I blow a kiss into the air and hope it finds him wherever he is. Tomorrow we are going to a place I have always wanted to go but not alone.

One of my true friends, Janet, likes this place so I will see if he follows me in. She claims that you are carried away to another dimension once in there. I am taking her suggestion to heart that I bring a man with me. If you go there alone it is not as powerful. Janet is always in her gardens planting, pruning and producing most of her food and beautiful flowers. She has been called a lady of a thousand smiles and I agree. If only more people enjoyed the simple things in life, like smelling the flowers.

This could be the start of something I have been looking for. The days go by so slowly sometimes with very little to stimulate the brain. I love my computer and use it every day. My dream had always been to be a writer but nothing to write about really. The days flew by when there was a family, meals to make, floors to sweep and never enough sleep. It is amazing how age sneaks up on us. Maybe an illness can

also slow you down but either way, we notice the changes. I may

have health issues but life is to live and I feel stronger today.

Three A.M. wake up

TICK...TICK...TICK...I hear my clock ticking as I lay in my bed. "
No, I do not want to wake up yet ". There is no noise outside so it
must be real early. I do not want to open my eyes to look at that clock
but I will look anyway. " Oh no, just three thirty " but I feel rested. It
must be that I am just happy about yesterday. What a man.

" I must get to that bathroom on my own " as I hold the bureau with
one hand and reach for the bedpost. I always feel less than sure
footed getting out of bed. My bathroom light is on all night because I
need to see where I am going. In the dark, it is just an accident
waiting to happen. Soon I will have to turn on that little heater to sit in
here once the winter arrives.

I suppose if I turned my heat up higher, the place would be warmer
but I can not break my lifelong habit of turning it down at bedtime.
These little disc heaters are perfect for instant heat. There is nothing
worse than a cold bathroom.

There were days I remember as a child when I was covered in an
old heavy quilt sewn from the pockets of men's suits. It belonged to
my great-grandmother and she gave it to my parents for a wedding
present. It was well worn but I could feel her hands holding me in it.

Even now, I guess I am like a child dragging around an old blanket forever because it still graces my bed as a cover, tonight. I look at the stitches and touch them to imagine being there, back then. Memories are made from so many things like an article handmade by a long gone loved one.

When I was a very young girl I was raised in a small village outside of Boston, in Sudbury. It is next door to Concord, Lexington and is located on the main highway during the Revolutionary days. It was called the Boston Post Road which headed west across the frontier to New York. The first real place to rest for the night on a traveler's journey was the Wayside Inn. It is still there today.

The old Inn offered rooms to rent and a lively tavern open to the weary traveler whether they be rich or poor. All drank grog, a homemade type beer but the important or better off person drank cognac, madeira or applejack, made on the property during the harsh winters there.

The process was simpler than brewing, just fill a large barrel with apples to the top and seal it closed and set outside in the snow and ice. Then once a month you chip open the top lid and scoop out any ice you see formed in there. Each time you seal it down again and repeat the process until spring. The liquid that is remaining is a pure alcohol because the water in the apples has frozen and now is removed. The apples were fermenting in a frozen state because alcohol does not freeze. Leave it to our ancestors to stumble onto that trick.

My first dream was to be a writer and fall in love with a boy that read my book and wanted me for my intelligence. That must be an early defense mechanism when you know you are not

perfect like all the other kids are. I would ride my bike there with a small lunch and my diary with pencil.

Who would bother a dreamy eyed girl sitting under a tree writing in her book, a diary. I know that Henry Wadsworth Longfellow stayed at the Inn many times and his most recalled work was written there. I only remember the beginning. " The ride of Paul Revere " I tried to write a poem but my experience was limited back then.

I would ride next door, across the Dutton Road, to sit on the giant rock to read the poem on the metal plaque there. I was sure this could inspire me. Behind the rock stood a little red schoolhouse from long ago. A visitor could enter to see the tiny chairs and desks with the school teacher's desk in the front of the class. There is one blackboard with the alphabet written in chalk. The room was heated by a very small wood stove and only a dozen books are on the shelf. I remember looking out the window at the little, red outhouse too.

The glass was wavy and looked thick with bubbles in it. Then you go outside to read the poem embossed on the metal plate secured to the stone. It begins " Mary had a little lamb, it's fleece was white as snow, and everywhere that Mary went, the lamb was sure to go, it followed her to school one day, it was against the rules ". I used to think that Mary was still there and would help me become famous like her but nothing happened.

My friends all said that the Inn served mutton every day, they were being mean trying to say that the little lamb was eaten ! The town has a zip code of 01776 to secure it as the home of liberty and commerce. That apple jack was a favorite of General Washington and his troops when they stayed there.

The face in the mirror looks back at me as I dream quickly of all the time that has passed in my life. I look the same as yesterday but now I feel prettier. How is it that my bad driving has led me to " bump into " Prince Charming yesterday. I am shivering right now but not from cold, no, it

is him in my mind. I am getting back into bed and get comfortable again. I always loved being in bed and more so lately.

It is easy to forget everything and just pass out but this early morning is different. The nights have been harder for me as I toss and turn while thinking over those little things that seem so big when it is pitch black outside. Right now I feel like I am on cloud nine and I have a silly smile on my face. I am happy for once.

I know he liked me and even though I was suffering from stage fright. I hope my mouth was not hanging wide open. I guess it was meant to be, a Twist of Fate, a Godsend, good Karma or just an accident that developed into this. I am not crazy to want a friend to share thoughts, looks and maybe more, with the right guy. My days are structured and normal when all at once, " pow ". A genie has

come out of his bottle and answered my three wishes, all at once.

This man, Ray, like the sun shining on me, made me feel wanted,

interesting and beautiful. The few things I wanted a guy to be like.

He certainly meets all those simple things and more. I thought I

might meet a man but not like this one. My feet are cold and my mind

is racing. I need my little footsies but I am too lazy to get them right

now. I do not want this dream to end even though I am half asleep my

body feels so alive. It takes something big to make me be this excited.

" I wonder if he is thinking of me ? " The girl and his sore toes.

Maybe he will forgive me and remember to never ask me to drive

when we go out today for lunch. He liked a place called " The two of

us " where it is clean with tables for two inside and out, on their back

porch facing the ocean. I will go to Burger King if he insisted but I am

never going to tell him that.

Ray called me a " Goddess " in passing when I said I have simple

taste. He finished my comment by saying " you have simple taste,

only the best " and I shook my head, batting my eyelids. I smiled,

crossed my legs and sat upright all at once because I like how he

talks to me. The nicest part about him I really enjoy is the easy going

but direct way he moves.

It is " yes miss " and " yes sir ", opening doors for ladies and

anyone with a cane. How many men, wearing a cap on their head sort

of nod and touch the bill of their hat to acknowledge you, can you bump into ? I did it because I am not perfect, my illness is slowing me down, so I needed that little buggy. There are no promises that can go unbroken in this world of human beings. I was hurt by my one and only lover many years ago.

He got in his car and left for the west coast with a tiny waitress from the next town twenty years his junior. Good luck to him I thought, you loser but my daughter, Mona was left without a dad. I did my best to be both parents for her well being. It is hard for a female to take on that stern, puffed up bad guy, that men can portray. I learned to be that way for the moment when needed and then I would start making toll house cookies like we made back in the Boston suburbs. Oh yes, Babe Ruth built his home on the Dutton road too. The greats of history still float in the air there and smile because the woods are still thick there, even today.

I think I will tie a small piece of yarn on my finger to remind me that this is not a dream later on our first real date. My memory is terrible if I am nervous and I will be but a happy, not worried type of jitters. When the meal is done and we are looking out at the sunset I hope the yarn will tighten on my finger, I will finally tell him to " kiss me Prince Charming " and after he is done I will toss away the yarn if he did not turn into a toad. That has happened before and I should have know it. I did feel empty on that date from Hell.

Whatever his name was, only talked about sports and cars which I do not care for and then he ate with both elbows on the table. He broke the last straw with me when he took my napkin and blew his nose, quite loudly in the middle of some fancy cafe. I could not wait to get out of there. It is a good thing I can text the letter H for HELP to my girlfriend Janet. I knew within a minute my cell phone would ring and she would tell me " her water broke ", I have to go right now.

He just kept eating and asked if he could take the rest of my lasagna home in a doggie bag ? I said " You betcha, have a ball ". The Hostess was smiling as I zoomed out of there, keys in hand, walking with a cane but almost at marathon speed. That fresh air felt so good. I thought I would pass out being with " goofball ". I am so thankful no one I know, saw me with him there. What a flop that was but this time I am so relaxed.

Ray said goodbye to me and I know he wanted to kiss me but he has manners. I am not going to wake up tomorrow night with that yarn still on my finger. A nice ring would look much better on me. I am going to blow him another kiss " good night " and close my eyes again. I want to wake up later like eight o'clock. This is my chance to pick out a nice outfit if I have the right shoes ? Oh no, you need to get up and get those heels on and walk around to test myself. I liked looking up in his eyes but I want him to know I am his equal but shorter. I have to stop worrying and let nature take it's course today. I will count the tic, tic, tics of this clock and dream of that kiss I want. I hope he likes it too. I have heard it is okay in this day and age to be more aggressive.

A sudden turn

" Today will bring some sun and then later in the day dark clouds
will form. We can expect rain by evening. Dug Scott, the weatherman,
with an On The Hour report. Next it is " Click Enough of you radio. I
am now wide awake. Why did I have to be aroused from a good sleep
by the weather and not a song. Any song ! Oh well. My bed is made
and it is time to eat. I want to forget my wild thoughts early this
morning.

The bright sun in this bathroom window reminds me that I like my
privacy and this quiet part of the day. A man will usually trash the
bathroom. The toilet seat up ALL THE TIME. Dumb guys say it is
easier for them next time they have to go. Who cares about females?
I am chilly and need to get going. Today is a big day and I want to
give it my best.

" Look at this wardrobe, nothing to wear. Oh what's this ? Yes, I
forgot about you. Shoes, stop hiding down there." This outfit is
coming together better than I thought. Finally I feel like I can be me
and wear something different and special. Today is better than a
lunch or a wedding because something good might happen. I want it

to be all I have dreamed about. He is so perfect this far just being easy going and a gentleman. I can not remember a man in several years that talked to me so directly but with a calm demeanor. I saw in his eyes a certain look that touched me. I am going to doll myself up today and use all my guns to maybe get this man. It takes an effort to do things and make it happen. I know I am not the best looking or healthiest person on earth but I know it is normal to want a soul mate.

My only romance was with my husband and high school sweetheart, Dennis. He was a rugged type boy but rather than play football to get the girls with a varsity jacket, Dennis got a job. He worked three days a week delivering groceries to the town's homes. This built up his social skills learning early to be proper in the presence of others. I recall he told me of the homes like his but others like the Munsters lived in on TV, There was an old woman sitting in a chair that smiled as they left the bags on her kitchen table.

The last time they were there she only looked down as she prayed to her rosary beads. He felt that she knew she was dying. He read the obituaries and saw her in there, died late yesterday. I know it matured him beyond his classmates. His proudest thing in high school was the ham radio group and the chess club. He said he might have been a football player, won a scholarship and later graduated Harvard d but took a different road.

The job built his body up to be strong as a bull with the control to be in a china closet. When in our last years together we moved apart but Mona kept the family together. We were both just innocent kids back then and love, marriage, family are words in the end. He wanted to see more, do more before his life was over, like all of us feel at times. I had a real love for him as the great guy that stood by me for all those years and like a bird wanting to fly, I opened the cage door. He has visits from Mona and her boy, Torin. They live in Clifton with her husband's family and the farm there. I might just have to go there with a new friend next time. The journey by car might be very romantic too.

I know I am building him up in my mind. This Romeo might be Doctor Jekyll too. Remember what Sandra told you " Bring your Mace and be ready to use it if he tries to move too fast or does not understand N period O period. " She is one of my friends able to read between the lines plus good at using her head first and not letting her softer side, the heart, rule the brain. I know she is right so often because guys do usually want just that one thing. I feel like I have Sandy on one shoulder telling me to " be careful " as she pokes her little pitchfork at my ear and on the other shoulder is Janet. She is like a tiny living angel of trust, love, beauty and sexuality.

I hear her whispering in my ear in her low voice like an old wise woman saying " Use your power over him. look in his eyes then look down quickly, purse your lips and then ask " Do you think I am pretty ? ". This is driving me crazy. I have to get going and stop daydreaming like this with my two little friends talking to me. Remember Etta Mae, you are the boss.

Ring ring, ring, ring, "Hello this is " click. Dialtone.." Let me see who that was on this caller ID ? " Baker, Allen.." Who the heck is that. I am going to redial this one .ring, ring, ring, ring. " Baker residence. Hello ? " . " This is a number you just called and then hung up on me as I was starting to speak ! " His answer was interesting. " I was calling a new lady I met and I could tell by your voice that you were not her.

There is no way to sound like a texan if you are not one. She is a cowgirl and my manners were poorly shown to you. I can only say that my hair is white, my fingers shake a little now but if you are single I owe you a coffee. I am sorry for the mix up but do enjoy your voice. I did not realize you had answered as I pressed End Call. I noticed my finger pressed a five and not four as the last digit I was supposed to dial. Imagine one number off ? If you ever are lonely or just hungry remember to write my number down. Goodbye ".

Well now I know another single man . This may be my lucky day after all.

It is twelve forty-five and I just noticed a car in my driveway. Yes, it is Ray and although he does walk with an obvious limp I see how erect his posture is. I remember now he was wearing a ballcap with a star on it and ARMY in larger print. He does look like a soldier carrying those flowers. What am I doing ? Get to that front door. Knock knock.

Hurry up silly and get this door open. I step back a little and here he is. My eyes move from his shoes which are shined and then up his front to the top where his smile warms me and then he says " I am early, do you mind ? " " No, I am ready, just let me grab my bag and umbrella as it may rain later ". " Etta, I was thinking of you in the middle of the night, all good things but I was still tired until I saw you. You look fantastic, smell so nice and I am so lucky to have you as my date today. Let us go have some fun ".

I locked my door behind me and he offered to take my hand as we walked those few feet to his car. I liked it right away when he opened the door for me in a casual slow way rather than hurried like he is thinking. " come on BABY, get you butt in there ". I buckled my seatbelt and he did his as the car started. It was neat and clean in his Buick. I like the roominess of the car. I turned to say to him to be careful of cars racing down my street and sure enough zoom, one goes by. We both smiled and sort of chuckled both knowing our first date could have ended up in the hospital or worse.

The traffic on this road has increased lately but it is just because of a detour nearby. This road, SpyGlass Hill, is still a country road. The winter makes it impassable at times except for the Jones family. They always had a team of draft horses to haul the buggy or a wagon down and back up the hill while laden with passengers or goods. The care given to them was the best in this county and even further. The older villages told me of the time a newborn was ill and the master of the big house took out the team in a " Northeaster " to fetch the doctor and deliver him to the door of the worried parents. This child later grew to be the caretaker of the stables at the big house. I am told he led the caisson through the village to the family plot. He was also the graveyard tender and dug his hero's grave the day before.

The thing I like about Ray is that he has this sort of " I am special to me but you are too " attitude or air about him. I looked in his eyes and thought out loud " forget the yarn ", which I had forgotten anyway. I put my hand on his neck near his chin and turned his head towards me and like a pitcher I scored a homerun. This kiss has been waiting too long to happen. Oh my, my, my, I do like this but it must stop and I pull myself away. We girls have to remember we can bring a horse to water but we can not make him drink but if he does start drinking it is hard to stop them. Kisses are the same as drinking water, they taste so good..

Remember what Sandra said about keeping one hand on the little Mace container. It looks like a big lipstick case. I had one hand on his cheek and the other on the button about ready to blast him if he surprised me. All I know now is I hope I can hold it until we get to where we are going. It is a beautiful sunny afternoon and I am with a man interested in me. What else can I ask for ?

I am not that hungry right now probably because of all the butterflies in my stomach all day. There is a small mini mall coming up on the right and I suddenly ask him to pull in and park in the middle of the front row. I am never this pushy or spontaneous but it came out.

He looked at me without saying a word but with wonder in his eyes. I said to him " you picked the place we will eat at right ? " he replied " well yes but I am flexible and will go anywhere you want to especially on our first real date. You know that ." His smile is all I wanted to see.

I pointed to the place right in front of us and I said " I have always wanted to go in there but was afraid to do so alone or with my best girlfriends. They have all gone in and said it is ok. " You will come out of there different than when you went in ". That thought worried me the most but I am opened minded and have inner courage. I never take things too seriously but this occasion demands it. " Follow me Ray " as I take his hand we walk into the Madame Betty's House of The Future.

Betty is an older gypsy and in her eye catching outfit she calls to us to enter " come in my children and sit in front of me. I was gazing in my crystal ball just now and could feel you both coming. The stars are aligned in the heavens above. Let me read your palms to understand each of you. Is there Love written on them ? Will you both be on the same paths. Please each lay your hands on my little table under this light so I may study you. I can see the color of your skin and tell if you are healthy. Your nails tell me how you feel about yourself. When I hold them I will measure the strength of your heart.

Do not let cold or hot hands deceive you. I will rub them gently and let your pulse talk to me. You two are here to see your future. I can see into the future for you. The past is already written and you know all the secrets held there. My eyes and my hands will use the glass globe to answer your questions. Your hands speak to me and my Tarot cards will warn us of any dangers ahead in your future. Relax now you two beautiful people and we shall all know what is to come.

Finally Madame Betty closes the drapes and locks the front door before she is ready to begin. Ray and I both look at each other nervously. I have a past and so does he but is this a glimpse into our future ? I jump, startled at a loud crack of thunder outside as the rain starts pouring down on the roof. I turn to Ray and ask him " Is this too creepy for you ? " He replied " Not at all. This is what you really wanted to do and I only hope she does not put a spell on me like the old song says. I am not going to drink any Love potion number nine either."

He then asks one more thing with a very straight face to the gypsy woman. " May I ask how much this will cost us ? I want the deluxe deal . All you can do for us ? " she answered back thirty dollars young man, about the same cost of a nice meal later if you two still like each other ". I thought out loud, " Are there wedding bells in our future? " This made the gypsy smile and laugh before she answers " I will give you the good news , the bad news and what might be.

Nothing is written in stone when love is involved. Yes, you may marry but will it be this man with you ? Will he love you and yet not live with you ? Can you recognize the signs that point the best way for both of you ? You both must be like a leaf in the Fall. Ride on the breeze and end where you may. You will never forget this visit with me. My knowledge goes back in time. My people have held the power over good and bad if we know of it."

the gypsy Madame Betty

Once we settled into our seats I had a chance to finally look around. This is her living room or parlor as my dad would call it. The candles are in glass bottles and on candlesticks giving off that soft light that no bulb can imitate. The air is filled with a potpourri of scents that instantly relaxed me. There is a magic in the air with the aroma therapy and this mysterious ambiance. The round table in front of us looks solid and old. I looked under it to place my feet together and saw the carved faces of old women laughing. I pulled my toes back a little, " let them eat Ray " I thought.

The tablecloth is one of the finest I have ever seen. It must be from old Europe. This home is very clean and well adorned with antiques. I love the tall vases she has with plenty of flowers to further soften the experience. I can tell it is all done to move us into her world of the past, present and the future.

I am finally ready to let her look into our futures, this man and woman before her. Little does she know we were strangers yesterday. I know secretly I hope to hear all the right words. " You two will live forever in love, deep love. No other will come between you for eternity. The future looks good my children." I am not the only one coming here to a soothsayer to learn my fate or am I just a fool with another one holding my hand as we face her.

The gypsy positions herself across the table and then she says to us " I will now read your cards. It is often said that it is " all in the cards " and I will use them now once for each of you. Be quiet and concentrate on the cards that show their faces. I do not control them in any way or as to what they say. Let me begin by doing both of you quietly without any remarks. If I laugh or sigh it is just me reacting to the story as it unfolds about you and your future. When I have finished with both of you I will read your palms and then conclude with a look into future with our eyes.

Suddenly Betty takes out her cards from below the table and shuffles them quickly while staring into my eyes almost without blinking. Then she starts to lay them down in a formation like a solitaire player might make. Then under each column, she slowly and methodically positions the new card from the deck.

Next, Betty puts the tip of her first finger on top of the card and tapped on it as her lips moved silently as if she were talking to it or herself . This was followed by many more cards and sometimes a groan from her as she covered her eyes and shook her head side to side. I never heard a word but I felt doomed when she finished my turn but then she looked at him.

Ray was just sitting there watching all this and taking it all in. My mind flashed forward to ten years from now and he tells a crowd about our visit to Madame Betty or maybe tomorrow telling his men friends that he met a kook on a date to the fortune teller. Either way he was now the subject of Madame Betty. She shuffled and shuffled, five times more, while never taking her eyes off of him. I was starting to perspire just watching him start to sweat profusely. It was actually funny but I did not laugh at this important moment. I hope she exposes him if he is a fake and bad for me. If she has powers use them now gypsy lady. Zap him if he deserves it.

The cards are finally laid out on the table but this time she is giggling and holding back tears being amused by his cards. I could see devils and ghosts and other terrible things, on the faces of those Tarot cards, but his reading is all happy and wonderful while mine was doom and gloom. What have I gotten into ?

All this time she has been silent as she study's us like my primary doctor, Doctor Judy, does and in a similar way. There is silence except for the similar moans, groans and other noises I am used to hearing. The grand finale to this experience begins now. We sit back and she puts a box on the table and I notice how ornate and carved in wood with the words - Here In Lies The Future.

Madame Betty opens the lid and lifts out the round glass globe. It is shiny and polished and the light above glows on the surface but able to penetrate into the center. She holds it in one hand while gently closing the top of the box. Now the piece is placed on top of the lid, in the center and fits nicely.

It is at eye level and she now sits and speaks. " I will look into the future. My hands will circle it only an inch away but the electricity on my skin will effect this perfect circle of glass and tiny particles of lead. It is imbedded in the glass to strengthen it and make it glow. I could feel her feet rubbing the carpet below.

Madame Betty moved her shoulders up and down slowly letting her silk robe create static electricity. She then explained to us " Now I want you two to put your heads closely together with your faces about one foot from the glass ". We did as she asked and then she moved her face to within inches of it but across from us.

This was like a magnifier but also like a mirror in a fun house. The views were distorted and to add to the confusion she started to speak in a high pitched voice " You young lady, need to watch very closely to what I show you and you, young man may see things in there you want to see but do not ignore other visions before you. Suddenly Madame Betty starts to sing in a much lower voice.

" The horse travels many roads and jumps the brooks and walls. Remember, that a swift sure footed horse is made complete when ridden by a true friend ". She asked us to now watch the glass closely. I saw her face move up to the glass and then kissed it on her side.

Almost instantly there was a white, foggy background now hiding her image and somehow I thought I saw something moving and twirling. I squinted to make out an image when suddenly I saw an old sailing ship, rocking in a rough sea. The image fades away to that swirling fog again. Next two horses appear pulling an old buggy with no one inside. The last image I recognized was that of three hands clapping each other. Just as suddenly the globe became dark and I saw nothing but I noticed Ray was looking intently now into it.

He never moved but his eyes blinked fast and then were wide open. Could it be he sees something I do not ? After pulsating as a bright light it changed back to glass with tiny sparkles glistening at us. Could it be I went blank for a few seconds being so into the experience. Then without much fanfare she moved her little chair next to me, on my side, away from Ray and cupped her hands around my ear. This psychic, Madame Betty, then spoke in that spooky high voice but very slowly and softly.

" You are in very good health and the future is bright. Your hands have lines that are deep. The line of love is strong and healthy. If this man is of interest to you I will condone it but remember that my view of the future will be if both sides are true to each other.

I laughed at his cards because he faces things with courage and will get up if he falls.You have had many sorrows and tears. The cards showed me that but also that you are a strong person on a new journey. It is fine to walk a few feet a day with someone than to walk a thousand mile alone. Follow your head and your heart my child ".

Madame Betty moves next to Ray and I can hear her voice but it is strangely much lower. I think then that Madame Betty knows that a man will listen to another man any day of the week before asking a woman car directions for instance. I feel like I am watching a reverse confession, the opposite of those at my Catholic church.

He smiles the whole time and I am happy to see that because we are done here soon and I am hungry. I would think Ray is too. She moves slowly to the door, unlocks it and then opens the curtains and drapes. " I did not want the outside looking in. Good bye and come back again ".

We hurried to the car and I had to ask him " Do you hate me or think I am weird ? " He shook his head saying no while speaking slowly in his deepest voice saying " Madame Betty knows all and tells all. She told me you were a good woman and if ever she acts oddly just accept this and there will be peace in your life. " I was surprised she said all that and then he added " If this is a first date be sure to not take her where you want to eat. Go where the wind blows you .

Ray and I both started laughing about the whole experience. How many other couples would do it ? Maybe on a first date is the only time he might agree. I know if he wanted me to go the car races with him I would do it, once. I think a couple should do many things together to learn more about each other. Just because we met by accident and hit it off does not cement a relationship. When you disagree becomes the real test. I know that my desire is for a good guy to like me and just be company when we feel lonely. If it becomes even more than that I will deal with it. This guy likes to do more than just sit on the couch in front of the " boob tube ".

The diner to eat

The day has been memorable with our visit to a fortune teller finally over. I wonder what else Madame Betty whispered in his ear ? He never stopped smiling slightly but I noticed a grin once or twice. Maybe she could read minds and see the future but not me. He is just driving like we are heading somewhere we had decided on. " Ray, are we going to eat soon ? You had mentioned the Two Of Us place and it sounded romantic. Are we heading there ? "

He glanced at me and then back on the road then said " I liked that lady. It was like going to a movie but we were the stars in it. I am not so sure I liked the part about the end as she described it to me. The last thing she told me was not to go where my first choice was if for a first date.

She said your foolish buddies heard it was a hit with the ladies. Remember not all women are impressed by Wedgwood plates or flowers on the table. You should go to your favorite place, If you can be relaxed like you were home together having a cozy dinner, the better you will be. Concentrate on her and have no distractions. Be yourself and nature will take its course ".

That explains why we are heading out of town and into the country. The next town is twenty minutes away. Oh well it is a nice ride and I can enjoy this new adventure today. I suppose seeing Paris, Rome and the Egypt are something to talk about but maybe it is the simple side of me to like little things. I want to ask Ray another question about the Madame but maybe it is best to wait. He is humming to a song on the radio I have never heard before.

I am going to soak up these moments together as we make memories. My other girlfriend Jayne suggested that when she goes on a date that she lets the guy eat in peace while just sitting there. She said to think of him while you are there and then do something about it. I have to agree about one other thing she swears by that the way to a man's heart is through his stomach. If he likes your cooking then every night he will be home for his special meal you make each day of the week. Otherwise he will eat out often and live off of the Daily Special menu. Another tune I have never heard before but I am getting comfortable and I think I will shut my eyes and take in the breeze.

The next few minutes went by swiftly as I recalled the gypsy lady and all she told me. I know she was not a doctor but when she said that "as I press my thumb into your palm three times I then see the color return quickly. The heart is that of a child ". The part that bothered me was not the most important thing but it hurt the most. She said that I will have to finish growing and to be that great person that is within me. How did she know I was insecure about my life, my loves and my future ?

Maybe I was slouched over with my mouth wide open when she looked at me directly or how my voice was nervous sounding after she spoke in that witchy voice. I admit she was really a person to notice. The room was done in Victorian drapes with braided ropes for the sash.

The sitting area, before the readings, was comfortable. There were books on the little bookshelf by Lovecraft, Shelly and titles like Astrology, Curses and one on the Super Natural. It appeared to me the lamps and tables were very old and I would think these were passed down to her.

Most of us keep a few things that are precious to us. My mother's colander hangs in my kitchen like a million dollar heirloom but it is really a million memories. Another thing I liked that Madame Betty said was that I should remember things mother taught you but never forget to be your own person.

I know we all do not have memories of a mother or a father because of different circumstances. It is easy to look at a big family with the father, mother and four children. The faces all have some matching feature that links family members. Our personalities may be developed from childhood and be a learned behavior but the real core ways of acting just show up at times. One child may be shy and quiet like mother or if dad is the mellow one. I want to be the stronger person now.

The car comes to a stop and he shuts off the motor. I open my eyes and look at him. " Are you awake yet ? " I answer after a quick yawn " Yes, was I out long ? " I know I was just resting my eyes but then he says " you slept the whole ride here and I needed time to think about what we can do next after we eat. Here we are at my favorite place to eat. If we become a couple or not I will still eat here. " I turned and looked to my right. It is a shiny, chrome old fashioned style diner called Ted's Diner.

I liked the looks because it was clean and well maintained on the outside. " let me bring you inside, it is a nice place and we can talk in a booth together ". That sounds good to me as he opens my door and I get out, after he slides the door to the left it disappears into the wall except for the handle. I walked in and fell in love with it. There was chrome and stainless steel everywhere. The ceiling was rounded like we were in a dining car on a railroad trip on the Orient or the Istanbul Express.

I definitely approved of the cleanliness in general. Ray motioned to me to the left and into the last booth. I sat down with my back to the wall so I could admire the place. This was another thing I will scratch off of my bucket list. There are three older men at the other end having coffee and it looks like dessert from here plus four teenage boys at the other far end both. It must be a man thing because as Ray looked down at the men one guy saluted him and another winked at us. That was it Ray said " Do you mind moving in more ? " He moved in next to me. I think he was showing his manhood to me and to them.

The waitress came right over and laid down one menu in front of me. I thought it was odd but I just thought they were in short supply of menus. The offerings were fancy to simple fares. I thought the ravioli's with summer squash looked interesting and a salad melody. I like fish and chips too but let me see what he likes here, not that it matters at this point. The lady returns with ice water and then asks me " are you all set ?

I am sorry that I forgot to introduce myself first. I am Jeanne, a nice country girl, mother and grandmother. I believe in Karma and can tell you one thing, Ray has never been in here with a lady. You must be special. I feel good vibes from this table. I live happily with my many chickens at home and a man with a guitar to make music for me.

Life is good. So are you all set ? " That is when I had to say " What are you having Ray ? " Jeanne speaks up and says " He has the same thing every time he comes in here but it is always different ". Now I am lost for words as to what she means. Ray finally speaks up and says " What is the daily special ? " like he was the one just waking up instead of me.

Jeanne points to the sign Homemade baked mac and cheese with or without bacon bits and of course a large piece of Bumbleberry pie. He spells out b.i.n.g.o., bingo. She turns to me and again that instant reaction of failure to start brain before engaging mouth happens and I say " I will have whatever he has " and turn to smile at Ray. I would not make two separate meals if we were eating at home alone together. Even though we are here at Teds, I secretly love mac and cheese and must compliment myself because I make a mean meal but out of the box. I notice Ray is still eyeballing the guys down back.

He turned to me and asked if I minded him putting some money in the little jukebox in our both ? I said to go ahead and be at home. He dropped four quarters in and punched a few B' s and C' s when suddenly I heard music coming out in the little speaker here, next to me, plus the big real one down at the other end came on. The song title came up on the little display. The Beatles " You Know My Name " which I did not recognize. The bass was booming and the singer keeps saying in a thick British accent " You Know, You Know, You Know My Name Baby. Three times then he sings   Look up my number ".

This was all they could take. The group got up and left out the middle door while one said " Great song, you know how to get my goat ". Ray winks at him and says " that was the idea old man ". I can only hope he knew them. Here comes petite Jeanne with our two hot plates. The steam is rising off of them and within a few seconds she brings over two extra large piece of pie. She says " I will leave you guys alone while you eat unless you need something else, right now ? " Ray says " Yes, more salt ".

We had both ordered the same drinks too since I asked for what he wanted. She brought over one can of Moxie and he pulled the tab and drank a third of it. "Ahhh, like it says on the can Distinctively Different ". I had heard of that stuff as an old medicine drink great-grandfather Walter loved up in Bangor, Maine a century ago. Jeanne shook her head at Ray as she glanced at me. I was about to say okay when Ray blurted out " I like sweet tea too. "

That was it, we were " all " set as the waitress asked. My meal was cooling and as we both went to get a drink and fix a napkin a small problem existed. I am a lefty and he is a righty. Rather than change seats I left the man on the outside and I timed my bites in between his.

It worked fine without incident. He mentioned that he liked to eat a little first to get some energy in him. I felt the same way because I was drained earlier and a good hot meal with good company can not be bested by much. My first morsel until the last was like heaven. Real smooth cheese and ice cold tea went together well. We had the place to ourselves and if there is a next year anniversary from today we will be back for the daily special. He left Jeanne a big tip and told her to tell Mr. Goat to say hello to Mrs. Goat, the old couples real name.

We got to the car and Ray opened my door and jumped in now full of energy after that respite back into time at Ted's Diner. " Well, where to next, Ray ? I was ready for anything. That pie was still on my lips so I asked him " what is a bumbleberry anyway ? I grew up in a small city. " Ray replied " When they make apple, peach, cherry, blueberry, raspberry, blackberry and apricot pies, they put all the leftovers of each into one pie. Years ago people were called a " bumbling idiot ", in a loving way, for someone who messed up everything.

It was the best pie I have had in many years. I decided to mention to him that Madame Betty said " Walk together, hand in hand, among the crowd. It makes you come together closer and makes something of a simple walk. Then the madame said in her higher voice." There is danger in love but when hands touch the heart beats faster. I saw you two in my crystal ball as you sat across from me.

When your faces touched for the first time I saw your eyes and his eyes close at the same moment but both stayed that way for a few seconds. I saw two people enjoying each others touch. The glass showed me a long road ahead but the cards told of perils and chances of success and failure. " I have often wondered if these soothsayers and other mentalists really do know something we do not know. How would they know me or him but I liked it all and we are here ready to go on the next part of today. " what now ?"

He asks " do you mind calling it a day. I need to go home but I have enjoyed everything today with you ? ". I was surprised but said okay.

He drove me home and opened my door. Then we walked to my door and he said " see you tomorrow ? About five pm for dinner here ? " I said that would be great. He moved towards me and we kissed goodbye.

It was not a long one but it was sweet. Maybe it was a bumbleberry flavored one. Goodbyes were exchanged and I went in. The house felt strange and quiet as I changed into my at home outfit and slippers. My heart was dreading the thought of being alone tonight but then again it was a wonderful day. Who knows why he had to go home. I know I am going to jump in that bed and cover my head with my blankets for a few minutes. I feel like I might laugh or cry or both. Romance is never as easy as it sounds.

me, me, me

Now I need to go online and spread the word to my daughter and girlfriends. I will email them all about this day that changed me. A person can feel it inside when a moment is special. This guy attracted me already because of how relaxed I felt. It is normal for me to shy away from a man trying to speak to me. The world is so full of suspicious characters that I need to beware. This crazy thing called love is wonderful if it is right. Now the email.

I will start each with the same subject title " TWO TODAY " and in the body of the message area I will paste in the same words to keep it simple and make them want more. They are my family, friends and romance is important in our lives. Those of us that like to read, anything sometimes, crave new thoughts and shared experiences.

It is sort of like writing our books in letters now. Let me compress my excitement into just a short poem I will write now and then send. No one will publish it but they will know a nerve has been struck in me. Yesterday my comments were plain and just keeping in touch salutations. Now I will try my fingers on this computer to be creative and expressive. They will all love it whether it is good or not. It is the thought that counts, to be included in another's life, plus hearing me express my feelings

Let it be known near and far

that two hearts race, now, at my place

as I leap headfirst, into the great unknown

That was fun to plan each word into a poetic form but I believe the skills can be learned. My mind has always been drawn to words in stories more than verse. It is a true art to be a poet and " I know it so I hope I do not blow it ". Imagine I recall that from a Dylan song. Maybe someday I will be moved enough to write things. I have always wanted to do it but I suppose it is the fear that no one cares about what you say.

" Your cousin Kenny is gone. He passed away last night at the Veterans hospital ". That is all the message said. My sleep had been so deep I heard a phone in my dream but could not get to it. You know how dreams are strange, things seem to be real until we wake up. The phone showed a new message, Her voice was calm and clear with that hint of a Rhode Island accent. It touched my heart to be remembered and informed of this. He lived a life of his choice and served in the Navy for five years. I was always proud of that.

I looked into my contacts list to get my aunt's home number and called it. " Hello Aunt Charlotte ", my heart races a little because her voice sounds just like my mothers did. Both looked and sounded like twins. They were close and mothers death hurt her. Every day, like many of us do, they spoke at length on every subject. It was not just the weather and cooking, no, it was politics, opinions with a mix of reminiscing. Their oldest sister is the grieving mother, Catherine, living in an assisted living home.

Imagine being ninety four in a few weeks and while in a home for two years she now has to face this. The very elderly have that common tragedy of seeing their children pass away. Kenneth was the youngest of four and I am told they brought Aunt Grace, as we called her by her middle name, to his bedside at the Veterans hospital. She was able to hold his hand one last time and she talked to him. It was all about her love for him and the good memories she had. No one has time for negative or bad memories. I heard that he moaned only now and then at his end. That was a very sad phone call to deal with. We are a positive family and believe in moving on with our heads held high.

It is only seven thirty at night. I had a day all crunched into this morning and lunch. I wonder if he will call me tonight ? No way am I going to make more out of him than what he shows me. I refuse to be desperate and chase after him. I believe we should be after each other in that tango for two, perfect courtship and still a fragile union.

I still have Madame Betty speaking in my ear, sort of, because I hear her words and those odd voices she used. Did she tell Ray to hop on his pony and to giddy-up, " Get outta Dodge ? " The truth is I am a skeptic of those things she did but being there in her lair I felt entranced and a willing participant. There is no doubt her warnings and advice were common things for her to say.

I want to believe her observations were accurate like a third party person sizing up couples. The place and her mysterious ways did add to her power play. When she halted her sentence once and said " Do you really want wedding bells ? It can happen if you play your own cards the right way " Now that made me feel powerful and in control at last.

My night is going to be short I think. It is as if I ran a marathon today, I suppose we all experience extreme stress on a first date with a real potential companion. It was refreshing to see Ray sweat while under the thumb of Madame Betty. He is a gentleman and a good Boy Scout too. The Army teaches all the troops to be civil and well mannered. She put her spell on him with her stare. If a man were doing that with him I think he would act very differently. I liked the way he chased Mr. Goat and his cronies out of the diner with an old Beatles song.

I have noticed he is a man of action but moves in a calm, calculated way. What lady does not like a door held for her or some other notice taken by a man. I must admit I stopped counting how many guys did that for me and I always acknowledge them with a " thank you sir ". This separates the queens and princesses who walk right by being so privileged and just silently ignore him. The real ladies are flattered and know he is not a slam bam, thank you, kind of man, he is a very nice guy. Ray is that way, from what I have seen. If it turns out that we become close friends and act like teenagers again then I am ready for it. I know having his company was exciting, interesting and quite funny. He eats the daily special there, at the diner, all the time.

The girls like Jeanne there must like him and he gave out three Madame Betty business cards. Jeanne gave us excellent service so next time it is the " quiche " for me. She is so pretty with a nice smile. There was a very alert but fast paced way about when she moved. She is a woman in love, her glow was obvious but it is not for Ray. She left us alone with our food, the jukebox and bumbleberry pie. I want to go back there all the time too. If Ray wants to eat here then that is fine but if my too much salt incident happens again I will give in and go out more.

I am not really hungry but as I open my refrigerator, I spot that piece of pie, that Ray insisted we each take home to eat. I can savor this part of our funny encounter. He was right. My kettle is about to whistle for my hot tea to wash down this pie. The different choices, of fruit, with each fork full are like little still life paintings. It makes my mouth water just looking at it. I will sit here and enjoy this surprise treat while I rethink the day. I opened my kitchen window half way to let in the fresh night air. It is getting dark in the room but I can not stand a bright overhead light unless I am cooking.

I could turn on my little table lamp here but the moon is out and almost full tonight and casts a nice glow. I see it reflecting on my pie plate. My favorite dessert dish was my Mother's and I remember her with honor at tea time. We all love desserts that are interesting. There are a few of us that are the vanilla only type personalities. This pie is out of this world and as I am about to finish it when my attention is drawn to my neighbor's house next door. Every light is on downstairs and up too. I know this is a voyeur behavior but I am in my house and not using binoculars.

I am only guilty of looking too long at what I see happening upstairs. Two silhouettes come together for an embrace, it seems to me. I should look away but no I want to see more. It is like a movie on television, sort of. I could tell they had now fallen out of view doing what lovers, I assume, do behind closed door and windows with see thru curtains.

I hope my face is not too red when I see Doreen and her roommate, Celia. They had better not watch out their windows or the shadows may be coming from my bedroom. This guy, Ray, tickled me deep inside and he was not pushy and grabbing me everywhere. That is relaxing to not be on my guard or fighting off a jerk, like my other neighbor Gene.

He is helpful as a fix it guy but that is as far as I go with him. If I have something I really can not do and no one else will help me then I break down and call him. Usually he ends up almost feeling me up as we put up a wall shelf. One day I realized he was on the floor looking up under my sink but he had me turning the water on and off.

Then it dawned on me he was checking out my pantys' color. I accidentally stepped on his, you know what and said, " dream on ". When I bought a new mattress for here I had to ask him to help bring it in and set it up. He has tools and did it plus helped me with the sheets. Then he said lay on it and see how it feels ? Like a fool I did it and as I started to close my eyes he fell on me, by accident he claimed.

He was right on top of me but did not hurt me. I told him to get off and get lost. If he were a different kind of person I might have let him have his way with me. Now I am glad he went away and I told him I now have a taser and will use it if he tries to force me again.

It is strange that my hormones seem to be roaring tonight. Just a dozen hours ago, I tossed and turned over what today would bring. It was a very special day and I want more just like it. Now is the time I will lay in bed and get into that new book that Sandra gave me to read. She called it a must read for those believers that men are like dogs. They will chase cars all day but if a female is spotted they get out of their little minds in heat. She recommends throwing a bucket of water on a guy before a date. " It will cool him off before he gets any big ideas " Sandra is single, I must add. Now where did I put his number ? I could call him to say goodnight .

a real date to remember

I went to bed last night early with a that new book to read, from Sandra, " How to Skin a Cat in Nine easy ways". It is really just a mystery where the family cat is the culprit. I dozed off and slept without interruption until seven am. My plan for today is to clean my house thoroughly. That means vacuuming every inch of the place and when that is done do the dusting. My sheets and blankets are heading to the washer. It is time I do all those projects I have put off. I have all day to do it. Cleaning is a task but when you are brought up with a broom in your hand you learn to use it.

What if I were to get company this morning. If a certain guy calls me about coming over for dinner I must be ready. Everyone has a different standard for the cleanliness of their home. The truth is I will drop everything if I want to. My breakfast was a quick lite one since I knew my time was ticking away. I had finished changing my bed, running the washing machine and vacuumed two rooms when the phone started ringing. It was Ray to my relief calling to apologize for dropping me off yesterday and leaving so fast.

He said something hit him right after we left Ted's and his belly was upset. He could not get home fast enough and claims he spent half the night in his bathroom. I thought it a funny guy thing when he went into detail about how it had to be a prank pulled on him by the cook. Even though he ate every bit of his two servings of mac and cheese it seems he thought the end of the last one tasted funny. He said " like maybe some dish soap was squirted in the bowl before the food was added and then baked !"

I asked why he finished it and he said he had no choice as you never should leave food on your plate and that bumbleberry pie was so sweet that he shrugged off the incident. He then added that he did see the scrawny, little geek that was the cook, talking to Mr. Goat and his two " old fart " buddies. Those are his words not mine. It was done to ruin his date and he said that jukebox is going play plenty of a certain Beatles song if they come in. He did not believe Jeannie had any part of it because she knows " what goes around, comes around

After all his conspiracy theories were expressed he finally asked me how I was and did I like our date that was cut short ? I told him it meant more to me than words can express. He then blurted out," good, do you want to go to an auction in an hour with me. I need some things to sell on Ebay ? " I guess he makes extra money reselling things worldwide.

When the auction is over around noon time he offered to take me to the county fair a few towns away. He claims to have been going there for years, did work there at times, so he has a scooter lined up for me to get around easier. There are crowds and long walks but plenty to see and eat. I like the horses and begged him to let me watch the " dressage " demonstrations.

When I was a young girl my life revolved around my animals and my membership in the 4-H club. The organization promotes living a good life, have a clean heart, to love and care for your animals. I had a goat and two sheep. The days always flew by when you have chores to do and then grooming my furry and feathered friends.

We had cousins visiting " from away ", as it was called, who watched as I sheared the wool off of my sheep. Suddenly both of them ran into the house yelling bloody murder that " Etta is hurting the little lamb ". All the parents come running out and the reality sets in showing the difference between city people and country folks.

Those kids learned where their clothing came from being on the farm that week. I was allowed to work the spinning wheel as we made the yarn. The real lesson learned was that farm animals are part of the family and each has a name. They are fed, washed, brushed and hugged plenty. Every child should be part of the 4-h Club and the Future Farmers Of America to know where and how all our food comes from. Where will we be if there are no farms?

If times get real tough in this country only the farmers raising food will survive. The cities will starve when the shelves are bare and no one knows how to till, fertilize, plant, grow and then harvest their next meal.

Back to the phone call and our plans for today. Ray said his most important event at the fair was the main show, The Flying Wallenda Family of high wire and trapeze fame are the premier attraction. They do not use a net, never will, he explained to me. My heart stopped and I wondered how they can be so daring. I said to pick me up in thirty minutes as I am almost ready.

We hung up and my next twenty minutes flew by but when he knocked at the door I was ready. " good morning Etta " I gave him a hug and a peck on the lips. We got to his car and as he opened my door for me I saw Doreen, my neighbor, in the window waving and smiling. I waved back and she blew me a kiss. Ray said to me " At least you have neighbors you are close to. She is a sweet woman although very forward and obvious about it if she likes you,   I said.

I am too busy for her right now and as Ray gets in I tell him to hit the gas. He laughs and says " you are the boss " I have never been to an auction. It is an estate type sale so I am interested. He seems to know plenty about antiques from the little he has actually said about himself. I need to pick his brain more and make him spill his guts.

I just want to know more, more, more. He pulled out a small magnifying glass and called it his " loop ". You must have it to see the fine printing and stamped names on old things. Nowadays most items have China in large print. I love to learn and all I have to do is sit there and listen to everything. That is easy enough. Ray said that he used to go to simple country " farm and household goods " auctions. Sometimes his friend John would pick him up in his truck so they could fill up the back of it, which was often done.

At first John might buy some old tool or cans of paint, while Ray would look at antiques and oddities laying around to check out....Ray said his main interest was inside where the food stand was and he could get two red hot dogs, covered in mustard, relish and chopped onions, a meal was made of it. Ray explained that is why he went heavy on the condiments because he also only did this if he was one of the first people in line there to use them.

So many old timers, farmers, potato growers, mill workers and ranchers were always there. All wonderful and down to earth folks but he did not want anyone drooling or have the frequent sniffles he saw in line. Lots of trees and allergies may have been the cause but who knows.. He said John always nodded in agreement as he studied the crowd..

The auctioneer finally said " let's go " and we followed him outside, down the rows of things on the ground, boxes full of antiques, junk, junque (high priced junk) and treasures to be found. Lost long ago, hidden somewhere or no one knows what it is, in their family. Trained eyes can recognize things of value. Ray explained to me that the more you saw things held up for auction, the more you learned from the description the auctioneer would explain to us. He wanted to sell it so he let everyone know what it was, its condition and he would start the price very high.

If he wanted fifty dollars for an item in the end, he would say quickly, " Can anyone give me four hundred dollars right now " ? He would wait a moment for a tourist or a newcomer to raise their bidding card, it has a number on it that you are assigned. Ray said to always wait to see if anyone bids at all but be ready to spring into action. The auctioneer blurts out " no one at four hundred dollars ?

Give me three, give me two, give me one hundred dollars folks, this item is hard to find., where will you see one of these again ? Remember people, this is old and old is good now, who would have ever thought it is the golden years but not for us. No, but for my old pitchfork, Martha's sewing basket or that toy my auntie never let me play with. This item here in my hands is one of those memories to someone, long ago, just remember that as we continue the bidding. By the way, did you try the American chop suey, the pecan pie or a whoopie pie, she has pumpkin flavored ones too. Half the money she makes goes to the annual Christmas party here for the kids each year. Bring your grandkids, it's all free that day.

" Now I asked for one hundred dollars and no one raised their card, can I get any bids to consider at this time? ". Now someone experienced and hardcore like Ray stands up to make his bid. He raised his card to bid slowly. It was a book of matches " BARRY GOLDWATER FOR PRESIDENT " (a 1964 piece of history and politics which I like too.)

Ray firmly places his bid " Five dollars Sir " The auctioneers' face gets red, the crowd is shocked and I am looking towards the door as I know this can turn the auctioneer into a raging bull. Silence in the room, no one even coughs except for maybe a burp outback from Granny. The pause is so long he has no choice but to yell " Sold to the man with the pretty lady by his side ". Ray told me on our way out later that he knew the auctioneer had a five dollar minimum bidding rule.

This was another experience I will not forget. I was very impressed with the knowledge Ray has in so many areas there. Many of the buyers would show him something for his opinion about the age or value. I was impressed just with that. I felt special when the auctioneer singled me out too.

" Where now Ray ? " He turned and said " Hold onto your hat because we are off to see the circus " I have friends there that are in town and I always go to watch them perform. I will introduce you to the high wire walkers, like Alex and his new bride, the trapeze artist. They are both in their twenties. He rides bicycles up there about three stories above the ground with no net. Then the whole troupe of Wallenda's get on the wire and do a pyramid three levels high while Alex and his father Tito, hold them all up while sitting on their bikes on the wire. The crowd is always hushed during each performance.

Ray and I found seats in the front row as we enjoyed the thirty minutes of death defying acrobatics and perfection. His young bride swings on the trapeze and then hangs upside down while swinging but only holding on by her leg folded back at the knee. The crowds roar and clap. The children stare and many must dream of being one of the aerial artists above us. When the show ended the performers come down and meet you if you want to. It is such an honor and a thrill to know such famous people.

Later as Ray and I were deep in the fairgrounds about to have an ice cream Ray spotted Alex and his wife with him walking towards us, just two regular, ordinary people among the crowd. He made eye contact with Ray so they came and sat with us. The men ordered food and I made small talk with her. What can you say to a person who risks their life twice a day, every day ? They have no fear, like we do, because they live and breath up there and never stop practicing. The guys sat down, Ray and Alex talked mostly, while we all watched the crowds slowly going by. The beauty of life is in the faces of strangers, like the catsup, mustard and hot fudge on their faces.

I must be a snob looking at them and thinking like this but I just love life. Alex answered all of Ray's many questions about the family and where they perform next. Then with a serious face Ray asked Alex " how can you just stop in the middle of the wire and do a headstand ? " Alex just laughs and says " I started walking on the wire at three years old. First one foot off of the ground and the headstands started as soon as I could do one ".

Ray again complimented the new bride for her great beauty, power and grace. Then he turned to Alex and said " But I am mad at you, Alex " . Poor Alex sheepishly smiles and replies " Why is that my good friend ? " Ray says " You were not only running on the wire up there but you were running backwards too. My heart can only take so much." We all laughed and shook hands goodbye. I knew that this guy, Ray, was more of a special guy that I ever imagined but I am learning.

We went on the ferris wheel before we left and I was so afraid I might be sick up there and that fool Ray was moving the seat back and forth. I told him " never again on here Ray ". He realized I was scared stiff and he stopped and held my hand until we got off that ride. The french fries covered in melted cheese made that memory fade quickly. The ride back to my place was interesting. We talked plenty and laughed often. I had to thank him for letting me enjoy another great day with him, whereupon he answered " we are not done yet I hope ? " I said we could go to my place and that is where we ended up.

Puzzling things

The night is young but we had been at the fair for over four hours of fun, food and holding hands with Ray. It was crowded there but so much to see as we strolled in and out of craft, food, forestry and a sundry of little vendors. I bought a nice shirt with horses on it, a treat to myself while Ray now has a hot rod muscle shirt. The sounds of everyone talking and laughing with a mixture of a dozen smells always present is hard to forget.

Even while I enjoyed the horse showing events there was the smell of hot dogs, cotton candy and manure. Right next to me sat Ray having those things quietly eating and totally involved in nothing else. I have determined he is like the old " chain smokers " but Ray is a " chain eater ". He stopped at a french fry booth, he calls them food joints, but we must wait in lines of hungry people ten deep. All of us waiting our turn and annoyed at the slowpokes, dilly dalliers and the guy buying for his family of six already sitting at a table with eyes and mouths wide open. The beauty of all this to me was the humanity of it.

Some of us like families and closeness although I know people too shy or introverted for this place. We finally get our fries with melted yellow cheese on them. Ray ordered a large order because I said I would share with him. He even was about to salt more but stopped and looked for my approval. I nodded yes to him. This is when the " chain eater " showed up. He leads me away to another long line to stand in while we eat the fries waiting.

It was perfect timing because we were next in line for our real meal he called it, a large sub sandwich with steak and cheese, smothered in greasy, greasy onions and peppers with a sprinkle of hot pepper from a shaker. I shook my head, no way Ray, that is all yours. This was fine but ten feet away I am standing there watching him eat that thing like he was a starving refugee. The grease running down his wrist into his shirt must have tickled his elbow but he kept eating until it was gone and you guessed it.

I was ordering a small hard ice cream cone with two scoops, one maple walnut and the top one black raspberry. I chuckled because he ordered a kids size soft chocolate cone and said " This stuff is very fattening so be careful girlfriend " I heard him but just looked at my delicious treat as I licked it and just ignored him staring at me. I thought to myself " let him sweat like at Madame Betty's ".

The first thing he did was hop out of the car and come around to open my door with a smile. " Why are you so happy Ray ? " he said " you did not get up and walk away when I said girlfriend, that is why " I said " thank you boyfriend, now let me put you to work at my kitchen table. I have five hundred piece puzzle to put together.

A tough guy like you can handle that, right ? " He smiled broadly, put his arms around me and then we headed into my place. He and I looked up and there was Doreen waving at us again. She opens her window just before we get inside and says " Who is that hunk ? Do you share ? Does he follow orders ? " I looked up at her and just shook my head up and down three times and then looked at Ray. He was blushing but waved back at her as he pushed me in the door.

It reminded me of the diner when he sort of pushed me in the booth before him to silently tell the old goat, that is his name Ray swears to it. I think guys have that macho ego thing. We girls just hold hands with our significant other. That is simple and not all tense like bulls in a ring together. He does not know Doreen like I do.

Too well, I must admit but I did not know better than to have too much to drink one night with her and the others at the all girl party. Of course Doreen the hostess was in her dominatrix outfit being playful with her little whip. She tapped me twice on the fanny when I had my back to her at one point. I turned around quickly to discover her and two other friends of hers were all sitting there admiring my backside like I was on the runway walk at a fashion show. I felt beautiful in a strange way. I do not think Ray will fall under her spell but I did, accidently that one night.

Ray shakes me from my daydreaming and says " let me see the puzzle, is it this one ? Kitty cats and puppies? " He was wrong and it looked easy. Oh no Ray it is a different one. I pulled it out of a bag. " This is it Ray, it is called King Ludwig's Castle, the Neuschwanstein Castle near Munich, Germany " Ray smiles and then says " I know it well because I toured it while in the U.S. Army, on leave and I recall Walt Disney saw it after World War Two and decided it is the castle that we all imagine one should look like. He then used it for the model of Sleeping Beauty's Castle. I was very awe struck with it in front of me. " We can do it " .I dumped it out and we began.

I really surprised him with a can of ice cold Moxie from my refrigerator. I knew he loved it so I called three grocery stores until one place had it, Walmart. I went and bought one six pack. That will keep him her tonight and for dinner, the " house special ", a nice lasagna I put in the freezer just for a night like this and a guy who eats like an army. The hours passed and it was all fun. He is pretty good at it too. He said back a million years ago all he had for entertainment were things like monopoly, chess, checkers, puzzles and playing cards.

These things are mostly gone now as old hat, old school and the old folks, pre-video, pathetic toys. Little do young people realize that it brought us together instead of all this one with headphones in both ears. How will they ever learn to communicate to others. It seems to be empty but they say online chats and messages are like talking and getting together but it is virtual only, not face to face, nothing but a way to avoid real socializing.

" Ray are you hungry ? " The look in his eye and that smile spelled bingo to me. I pulled out my knockout punch. He watched as I took a cover off of my first attempt at a bumbleberry pie. His eyes lit up and I said " It is all yours to eat now and take home the rest." He stood up and hugged me tighter than ever before and looked into my face. I felt his lips on mine for a moment and then he said " thank you my sweet lady. No one has thought about me in a long time. If this is better than Ted's diner pie I guess Jeanne will not see me very often. How are you at daily specials ? "

Then the thought came to me " it will be different every day when you eat here Ray " . I could see him taking it all in but like some animals eating their food this time I will just sit and watch him. That puzzle looks great except for the one lost piece we can not find. There are worse things to worry about. I made my boyfriend happy tonight.

After he finished, I wrapped it up to put back but he said " Time to go my lady. May i call you tomorrow morning.

We can decide what to do next. " I shook my head as I walked him to the car. He started it and beeped as he pulled away. " Hey you, Doreen here, have you forgotten me ? " I waved and answered " Never, never, never you very bad girl, good night " I locked my door and went up to bed. I did not look out my window tonight. Doreen still has a sort of power over me after all this time. I guess it was not all bad. Goodnight Ray , I whispered aloud.

I was remembering the first time I heard Doreen's name was at the thrift store down next to the old church. The lady working in there was speaking of a house on Salem End road where an old witch had once lived. The village history was new to me then so I was all ears while looking at the clothing. She knew I was casually eavesdropping as her voice raised slightly. It seems that after the witch died her little house was never lived in again.

It was on the original property of the first captain Jones here. When his great-grandson wanted a house of his own it was decided to build on the old cellar hole left from long ago. The yard still had apple trees and now a few big weeping willows originally planted by the poor, old woman .Many villagers still believed in the old stories of her being evil and a witch. The Salem trials freed her and the Captain and his wife became her benefactors. It is sad how a mob can lose sanity when unchecked.

The new house was painted in bright colors and his new bride was from a far away country of Brazil. She met her husband in Rio de Janeiro when he sailed there. They were both special and when their eyes met it was said the bells in the Rio Churches started ringing. He brought her back to America to live in the tiny village. He slowly taught her english and she never heard the word witch in that family. They had one child, a girl, named after the old woman Doreen, once the resident here. This child was exposed to the world and another culture at an early age.

When the parents both passed away from a sudden illness that swept through town, she lived there alone from sixteen years old but was trained well. Her mother was a lady with ten green thumbs. The yard was always full of plants, flowers and on the house were window boxes. The garden was huge compared to many folks in the village. This woman, Bee, worked from dawn to dusk, hand washing their clothing, maintaining the gardens and teaching her child to count. It is amazing how we can communicate with our hands and fingers.

Little Doreen could count and sort of used a type of sign language between them. The villages often thought she could not speak because she spoke softly and was hesitant. One day Doreen was almost hit by a car and that Bee, screamed, ran to hug her child. She then started yelling in her native tongue, Portuguese, all the way home. They all knew Doreen was scolded but no one knew what she said.

The word got around that she was selling fresh produce and they came. The garlic, brussel sprouts, potatoes and beets fed many and let her earn money. A hardworking woman sets an example a daughter will never forget. Poor Doreen struggled to fit in with small minded people. Her mother was called a " jungle woman " and her name was the same as the evil witch. Some children are cruel to others and I see that as a sign of a mean spirit. It just made her stronger and the Jones family name protected her from fools

Carolina lives next door

I am here in bed thinking about how everything changed next door when sweet Carolina passed away. Now her niece Doreen has it all to herself and that is how life goes on. My first day moving in here I saw the woman up in that same window that Doreen shouts from. When I first saw this huge victorian style house on this hill I was intimidated being in this cottage so close by. I was soon to learn all about the history of both.

I was settling in on moving day and the helpers had all gone home when a soft knock was coming from the door. I asked who it was and a woman's voice answered " it is your neighbor, Miss Carolina Jones. May I come in ? " I jumped up to let her in and meet someone from around here. " Come in Carolina, I am Etta ". She holds up a small picnic basket and said "Are you hungry and maybe tea for two ? " I smiled in approval. The place is small but cozy and fortunately the men left the sofa clear for me to now use. I motioned to her to take a seat and she did while putting the basket on top of a moving box still full.

I sat next to her and she gave me a hug and when I squeezed her slightly she moved closer to me. I felt like I was with a family member. She kissed my cheek and then proceeded to set our little table on another box. It was a small tablecloth and then two tea cups and dessert plates. I am no expert but these seemed to be very antique looking. I was impressed with the gold trim on everything and even the spoons were sterling silver. " I have a choice of ham salad, egg salad or bagels with cream cheese which were delivered just now for me to meet you, just like this.

I have not set foot in this house in twenty years since I moved into the big house when father died. This cottage was built for me and my husband right next door and if you look closely you will notice lots of windows on your house and mine so they could keep an eye on us and they sure did. I had drapes in every window on that side of the house. " We both giggled at the thought of that. Newlyweds need their privacy.

She explained that her great, great-grandfather had built the big house here because his dad had been a sea captain on a great sailing ship. When it was lost at sea his mother wanted a widowswalk so she could look for him every day. " Our family goes back to captain Jones of pilgrim fame at the Plymouth plantation ".

The village had been called The Witches Finger because the land jetted out into the sea. It blocked the access to the tranquil bay here and was littered with early schooners traveling the coastline. This is a special sort of lagoon with deep water, perfect for heavily laden ships to dock and unload. The old sea captain had been a young boy of ten on a local ship working as a cooks helper.

He recalled a huge hurricane was suddenly pressing down on them and shelter was needed. Just as the sky began to darken, the old skipper of that ship knew the coastline enough that he ordered them into this quiet, calm port to anchor overnight. The next morning after daylight they set back out to sea. This boy remembered the old salt saying, " a sailor's home, this would make, when not at sea ".

When he was grown up, this man worked his way up to own a small schooner, he then brought his new bride here to settle and have a family. All his deck hands came with their families. The captain's wife started the first general store on the coast when any ship could arrive in the early morning to navigate the jagged piece of land, the finger. This name was given to it because the captain and his wife refused to carry slaves and after the Salem trials were over they allowed the last banished " witch " to live here.

He had traveled the world and had seen hokus-pokus in one hundred languages and did not believe in that hateful thinking. The Jones family built her a new, little cottage with a garden, chickens and flowers to enjoy in her remaining years. The " witch " name was soon to go, forever.

The captain ordered his marines, hired watchmen, to pass by her home every night, all year to protect her from the real, crazy people. Some of the other villages named the shipping hazard after her. She was probably just an old woman that liked being alone. There are still stories of the captain, his wife and the former witch, would ride through town with their heads held high. The family tradition continues to this day.

The following year all agreed the ship and old skipper were gone forever. It was agreed to change the name of the village to Widow Port forever. The hill was originally used to look for the incoming ships as soon as the dawn came. The big house was put there for the family to live.

The son ran the business very well. He had the widow's walk finished in a fine way. She had hot water running up there for her morning tea. The love and devotion they had for each other must have been great as expressed by her devotion up there. She was the richest woman along the coast but it meant nothing to her. Money cannot buy love.

The most interesting feature was the enclosed spiral staircase from outside plus the secret entrance from her bedroom. Long after she was gone old friends would be allowed at dawn to go up for hot tea from China, in real china and all hand carried from China. The chairs and table were rattan material with a view of the port. The old woman had asked on her deathbed that " whoever lives in this great home must climb to the heavens at dawn to watch for the ship and the captain. My soul will rest in peace for eternity ".

I asked Carolina, if she might want to look around again. She got up and walked slowly through every room, all cluttered with my things now. " The place is full of my memories and will now make them for you too. " I sold it when I decided it should be lived in. One couple stayed here all that time and the wife was not very friendly so we never made contact. You seem so easy going, I like you already. " The housewarming party over, she put her china away carefully and then while leaving she insisted I visit her soon. " I could not think of a nicer thing to do tomorrow. You are a wonderful neighbor. Goodbye for now."

That night I slept on the sofa and looked out the windows at her house. She was correct. The view was perfect for watching each other. I did not see her in any of the windows and as tired as I was I could not care less, being dead tired. If she did look over at me there was not going to be much to see. I did leave the light on being nervous in a new house.

What a day it has been. I have a new friend already and she is elegant, educated and so much class. I doubt she has a tattoo or ever swears. Her heirs might have been sailors and knew every bad word from around the world but not the ladies of high culture. There is nothing preventing all classes of society to be informed and interested in everything. This Miss Carolina Jones is one of a kind in a real sense.

Once and then again I thought I heard a faint voice calling for help. It was almost noon time and I had been in the house but thought I might enjoy the fresh air while eating. " Help me Etta, I have fallen in my garden. Please come in the backyard."I yelled loudly to her " Stay still Carolina, I am on my way. Help is on the way. I raced to her front gate. It was a tall wrought iron black door. I pushed the thumb button down and the gate opened automatically. I ran down the narrow walkway to find her sitting in a bed of flowers. She was more tangled up in there than hurt.

" You made it my dear friend in the lover's cottage. It seems I fell off the walkway. Once I landed my foot went into the bush and a vine grabbed me like a hand might. I was trapped being unable to turn over." I could see that she was exactly right. Some invasive plant was tangled in with the flowers. It took me two minutes to free her and get her on her two feet. After I dusted her off she straightened out and smiled " I do not drink, smoke or swear and my gardener will be asked to cut back all these beautiful plants taking up too much of the walkways.

My grandmother and mother were planters and kept everything manicured. You will see every inch of the property is covered in all sorts of things. They brought in seeds from around the world to see if they might grow her. Winter is too hard on tropical things. After this incident it is time for a heavy pruning and manicuring or a broken leg will be next for me. May I invite you in ? " I shook my head in approval and followed her into the house.

The first thing that struck me was the very tall ceilings and the furniture was old but highly polished wood. The kitchen had pots and pans all hanging for easy access as well as tall cabinets in an old fashioned pantry. A trip back into time. " Come follow me dear and I will give you the grand tour." Each room was described to me and had a name that the great-grandmother had designated.

My favorite room on the first floor was the full library with a huge wooden globe in the center on the floor .It must have been very old, even I could guess that, by just looking at it. Carolina said that there were eight hundred books at last count and at least two hundred first editions. She knew the titles of all the classics and pointed to each. I said " One could get lost in here and never leave it ".

Little did I know that in six months she would be suddenly gone from us. Peacefully passing in her bed surrounded by the things dearest to here from mother, father and great-great-grandparents too. This particular day of the tour she took me up to the widowswalk. It was all glassed and screened in making it breezy and sunny.

She pointed to the chairs and little wicker table and said " Those are the original pieces put up here for great-grandmother to sit in and enjoy her breakfast, lunch and dinner some days. There is her old telescope that she would look into for the last two years of her life. She wanted to see the ship with the golden mermaid glistening in the distance entering the harbor. Even though we were five miles from the sea shore I could see ships way off in the distance. It amazed me that generations ago women loved their man and stood by them until they died. How many hours did she spend up here with tears in her eyes ?

The bedrooms were large and one room that later belonged to Doreen was another window to watch things from. The gardens and hedges, lined the walks, like some villa in a photograph. Carolina had several bouquets of fresh cut flower bunches, all perfectly placed. Like her grandmother and mother before her, the green thumb was passed on. There is one room that never changed and that was the art room.

I am not an artist but I certainly would believe it if it was said that a masterpiece was there among them. The last time Carolina spoke with me was a Saturday. She was having a guest over to be a writing coach. Her friend was trying to write a book but although she was an excellent speaker, full of stories, the truth is the first page was always the hardest to finish.

I knew Carolina well by then, her intentions were very honest and just the fact that a person was willing to try something was most important to her. Almost as an afterthought she said " My only living heir, Doreen Zunto (her mother's last name) Jones will be visiting me this evening for dinner. She does not realize that she is the only name in my Last Will and Testament.

All my other socalled caring relatives are never to be seen unless it is a birthday or a holiday, if gifts are involved. This daughter of my youngest brother has always called me, helped me for a month when I was very ill and alone. Her reward will be when my attorney, Saul, calls them together for the reading. Each will receive one thousand dollars period and the remaining estate goes to my beloved and caring niece Doreen.

In my own words he will quote me from the beyond " I want you to live in this house and love it. Your roots are here and you are surrounded by the precious things that once belonged to me and other member of the Jones family. You and only you will receive the family fortune. It has been growing almost untouched in my lifetime. I cooked from scratch and mended my clothing. Not that I had to but I was taught to live that way.

My accountant assured me that you can spend up to one million dollars per year and with my hand on the estate until you die a trustee will release that amount on your birthday each year. Do as you please with your life and fill this house with laughter and things you might enjoy doing. I approve of this because I know you cared for me and now I can care for you."

We used to talk every day for a few minutes to say good morning. This was a silent way of checking on the health of each of us. On the second morning that I did not see her ,I called the police to check on her health and well being. Shortly afterwards there was a knock on my front door.

It was a police officer thanking me for alerting them. He said she was gone now and appeared to have died in bed reading or had fallen asleep. She had a copy of Moby Dick in her hand. I said " rest in peace my dear friend Carolina. I will watch Doreen for you now. "

I was soon to learn that the two were like night and day. There would soon be laughing, yelling, screaming and carrying on all night sometimes. This girl was on top of the world and in my mind deserved everything she now had. She earned it by being kind and considerate to Carolina until the end. I was surprised when she moved in a week later and said " I am now a dominatrix. You are welcome to my housewarming party next weekend.

I beg you to bring a few friends to add to the mix. This house is alive and ready to live. You are my special neighbor and I was told by

Caroline to always watch over you with my eyes and my heart. She told me to thank you for all the fond memories if she were no longer here to do so."

My first thought was that I will bring my best friends to this special occasion. I then sat down and sent out the invitations. I must have Sandra here to see this place. She is a bookworm and I think I know where she will be all day, in there, the library. Now I have the perfect reason to have Jayne over to catch up on the past and enjoy being together. I have to get Janet for sure. She will pass out when she sees that kitchen, better equipment and utensils than many restaurants.

I am certain Janet will teach them all something about the " garden to table process" . We will make an interesting ensemble. I wrote on each card to meet at my place and we will go next door to Doreen's place. The Dominatrix. That ought to get them over here to see this for real. Once they go in I hope they come back, still the same way.

The House of Doreen

This day is special because I get to see for myself what has been going on next door since it changed hands. Lately it is the constant sound of lawnmowers, painters, window washers and the distinct sound of horses. It is alive, for certain, since a young woman of thirty two years is in control now. The aunt, Carolina, had like many people getting older, started to slow down and let things go. I know I saw Doreen many times with Carolina in the windows " doing the spring cleaning " each year. It was done the old way with hand washing old lace and then drying in the bright sun, a breeze and hanging on the clothesline.

That girl would get out there when she was a teenager and beat those old braided rugs to no end. When she thought they were clean enough she would call her aunt who proceeded to walk over and whack that rug like a home run hitter. The dust in the air was all that was left because Aunt Caroline was walking away and shaking her head side to side saying " You are almost done with that one my love ". That girl was very strong and she was learning what it meant to be a young person doing things an older person has done plenty of times when they were able bodied. You are their little machine now, bought off by a nice lunch with ice cream and plenty of praise. There was always a five dollar bill on the table to go with when done. Now I will see how things in there have changed, if at all.

The first knock on the door is Sandra. These three special friends arriving now are my best choices of all those I know. They are all strong of body and mind. Each can handle a small crowd like I expect next door in an hour. I notice Sandra has a small bunch of flowers in her hand as she closes the door. The outfit she has on is tasteful and cut perfectly to fit her ninety eight pound figure. She is a deep person, very witty and quick. I found out that she was a retired judge in the criminal courts.

At some point in her career it was too much for her to waste a life dealing with mostly scoundrels, crooks, con-artists, misguided fools and some innocent ones set up by brighter criminals. The law business was good to her and as a favor to herself she attended the Johnson & Wales School of Culinary Excellence in Providence. She now cooks up all sorts of things and can mess up a kitchen in no time. The final things that end up on the table should be photographed rather than eaten. A still-life artist working in veggies, oils, pastas and wines. I like her along with us, it is like I have a big German shepard by my side. She is on the lookout for things that do not smell right figuratively and literally. The best seller, CROOKS and COOKS, is her first to be published. She is a nut for reading, learning and enjoying words arraigned in any way. I think Sandra will be a hit there with the quiet, in the corner, eyeballs moving quickly to the left and right crowd, when her nose does come out of a book.

" Have a seat Sandra and when the other two arrive we will hold arms, interlocking us and march next door like the Wizard of Oz quartet. " I said, while heading to my room to finish getting ready. Then Sandra asked " Well who is whom in this group, Etta Mae ? " I smiled as I stuck my head in the door so she could see my facial expressions as I answered.

We girls use our faces as much as we use words. " You are the Lion Sandra. You have great courage, we know that but you have the look of the King of the Forest. Jayne will be the beautiful Dorothy with the special shoes and beauty above most but still be just a simple girl. I remember in school that Jayne was wearing a big girl bra when we were all flat chested, playing with an EZ-Bake oven. I did not know at first that her looks and aura she gave off, drove some people crazy. I saw her running all the time after leaving school each day. She was pretty fast and I remember thinking that girls are better at running than stupid boys are. The truth was the boys were all trying to catch her.

She could hear them arguing with each other as to who was getting her. The dumb boys would never catch her because they were also acting in a teenager fashion. It was laughing, yelling, tripping, pushing and punching as boys do for any reason every day. That was the first part of the gauntlet done when a shiny new car would pull up with three beauty queen wannabes in a convertible. They would yell at her " Hey ugly. no boys will want you, freak. Your lips look like a big old fish, go kiss a toad, that is the only prince you will get." This hurt Jayne being a very nice, kind girl. She was a perfect daughter and did not deserve this abuse.

Then Jayne would stand erect with her hand on her hip, pushing her breasts out as far as she could and turn to look at them and say " Look in the mirror but you will never see anything like these, you surfboards ". Those same two of the three girls would jump out without opening a door and take off after Jayne again. It kept her in very good health. Now she is moviestar material, May West, Zsa Zsa, Marilyn and Madonna with a touch of Dolly Parton in one package.

She has no knowledge of any divorces that started when she hit the beach. The guys look at her walking down the street and are still smashing up their cars It happens when they take their eyes off of the road gawking at Jayne. Her blonde hair is a golden color really, with huge blue eyes that make some people go limp or for men, another direction. She can not help being born that way. I know her passions are being graceful to all, another lifelong bookworm and cooking expert too. Like many other beautiful people she knows looks are a curse sometimes and forces you to build yourself into a knowledgeable person. She looks and acts the part of a movie star, in my humble opinion.

Ding dong. The door bell announces that Janet is finally here. She laughs freely while saying " I am on time but just by a minute. Did I miss anything ? I had family to kiss goodbye to, nine grandchildren requires some chasing around the house. I picked some flowers from my mother's little spot. I see you all have your gifts too. Maybe we should put them together to impress her, right ? " We all put our flower bunches in the best vase I had and, " Shazam ", better than delivery. This will liven up the place. " The rest of us were sitting in the kitchen admiring each other and nervously awaiting this big party. Sandra says " let us begin our walk arm in arm, the tin man lady is here now ".

Janet never stops smiling and being happy and is ready to help anyone. She has descendants who may have been on the ships with Columbus. I have eaten her cooking and baking and it is out of this world. The recipes in her head alone would fill a file cabinet. I met her selling jewelry when she worked behind the counter. Her beauty, dark coiffured hair, perfect makeup and lipstick were what a customer wanted to see. When she held a diamond broach up to her blouse, it was always a sale in progress. I thought she had Liz Taylor like looks and it was obvious that was so because there were always men, young and old asking her to bend over to get this or that item from in the case.

She never thought like they did, as I watched an older man in his eighties and his son sixtyish, both straining their necks to look over the counter at her, rear end. Another beautiful lady but all heart, like the tin man had in the end. I guess I am the scrawny, thin scarecrow full of straw stuffing and little to no brains. I did stuff my bra too but that was tissue paper, back then. Finally I announced " Sandra is right, we will steal the show over there. She may call herself a dominatrix but we are not pushovers. I forgot to mention she has two cats, solid black twins named Shadow, the friendly one and Silhouette, the harder one to befriend. That is all I know from what Doreen explained out her window. I know Sandra and Jayne will be crawling under beds looking for both of them. They will acknowledge themselves no matter how picky these cats are.

I push down on the button with my thumb, like once before, the large gate opened automatically. We four walk into the front yard and our eyes are thrilled with rich flower beds and walkways lined with hedges. I notice two new white, life size statues, both men. Sandra points at the one of Michelangelo's David and says " My kind of man. A finely sculptured body, chiseled good looks and lips closed for eternity plus naked, rain or shine ".The other statue was also a David but the earlier, less know one done by Donatello, another from that period. I pull them up the wide front steps to the top. We notice to our left, five young, oriental woman sitting on some rattan furniture. They all stand together and bow slightly, at the waist, to each of us. We all return the gesture and feel instantly welcomed.

I ring the doorbell and we wait a few moments while adjusting our clothing and hair in the reflection made by the big glass, front door. Then it opens widely and there is Doreen like a new person to me. She is wearing a full two piece men's suit in white with a panama fedora and a big smile. " Etta, my one and only relative, my love and closest neighbor. You, gorgeous ladies should know you walk with an angel. You three are the cream of the crop when it comes to being her best friends.

Before we introduce you around I want to say that I have a couple of rules here. One is stay out of the cellar except for the wine section and beware if drinking from the large, leaded crystal, punch bowl. I can not monitor what goes in there or whom it may be to get in it again. This house will be full of fun, relaxation, happiness and learning. I want every room in here occupied by a special soul. I am taking applications for a translator, as you just experienced on the porch, plus I need a resident librarian, a lead chef, willing to teach others the finest cuisine, country styles from all places plus methods of preparation. She must also know how to cook for an army of starving villagers overseas by teaching those coming here to learn before going out in the world to save the less fortunate.

I want a male here to be the " man of the house " so to speak. He will not be mating with a harum here but will occupy the First mate's quarters. The carriage house is open again after many years being dormant. I have four horses in there now. A team to pull my antique, enclosed, four seater buggy that my great-great-grandmother traveled in. It was the finest made and still in perfect condition.

I dress in black with lace and a big hat while being driven through the village. I have heard that a rumor has started circling around that the " ghost of widow walk Jones " was seen, in her carriage, being pulled by giant black horses. My other two are Arabian bred and love to roam the one hundred acres of trails I own out back. It is funny but they follow the old trails, made one hundred years ago. Just remember girls that anyone that enters here is my invited guest. Stay a day or a lifetime. One last thing I must do is to introduce you to the Goddess in this house, Rania, the Egyptian beauty. She has climbed the Pyramids and kissed the Sphinx. Her feet have dipped in the Nile and her brown eyes and body have hypnotized many sheiks and their camels. You will all be belly dancing with her before the day is done.

Doreen notes that " It appears Etta has brought us another Goddess, equally as beautiful. There is always room for more of everything in this huge house. Now please move among all the guests and find your kindred souls. If a room captures your imagination then simply claim your spot. I only ask you are happy and willing to love others here and if you see my cats they are yours too. I am tired of their aloof attitude. Etta, you are free to come and go regardless what your friends do in the end. I must go to the basement to feed the dragons, trolls and lunatics. Just kidding. I only whip with a peacock feather she says while looking right at Sandra. We all laughed deeply and suddenly relaxed. This place is a home with many names now, Nirvana, Cushnoc or Potunk but a home of introverts, extroverts and those alone in their own world. My only thought is that I know I live next door but where will these three live tomorrow?

I was drawn to some beautiful pottery on a table and noticed that Celia was there explaining to a small group how she gets the white birch bark surfaces to her pieces. I begin to understand Doreen more and feel the need for a school like this. Special people spreading their talents freely and without stress. I ignored the others as they disappeared into the house. Celia and I talked and she explained that she felt gifted but her condition, being epilepsy, caused her to drop sometimes and Doreen is always there for me. That girl suffered

losses and ridicule from many but Doreen is a lover of people. I

realized then that the two shadows in the window may have been her

having an incident. I am ashamed where my mind went with it.

There were tables of fresh foods coming out of the kitchen, exotic

things and desserts. We all tried everything and ignored our waist and

bust lines. It was about four hours since I saw them disappear into the

big mansion. Suddenly I can see a plate of fancy Italian wedding

cookies being carried to the table. I hurry over to taste one. " Yes, I

thought so " I said aloud as I headed for the kitchen. There is Janet in

a large chefs hat and a white jacket showing twenty ladies how to

cook Italian style, old school ways. She had the five oriental girls

standing in a big tub crushing green grapes into wine. I heard nothing

but laughter and saw happy faces on everyone. I was proud my friend

was a hit. Now where are the other two ?

I headed to the library and sure enough there is Sandra up on a

roll around ladder getting a book on the top row. There are three

librarian types below her each holding two books for her. One asks, "

Are you ready to read to us Judge Rosecranz ? We want a romance

story please ". She answers down to them " I have a first edition book

by Bram Stoker, a love story about a tall, light skinned, man with fine

looking teeth. The character is named Dracula. This is my kind of

bedtime story ". I just smiled at the whole scene and now must look

for Jayne in this maze of rooms.

My ears can hear faint voices upstairs laughing and I decide to investigate. The art room door is closed, the sign says, " knock first before entering ". I listened at the door for a minute and I am not sure what to think. Doreen is saying " Faster please, I love it. My eyes are filled with beauty. " I hate to interrupt what might be happening, it sounds sexual but I knock lightly. I hear Jayne saying " Come in, my love " so I open the door slowly to look in. There is Rania laying on a long lounge chair with Jayne fanning her as Doreen shoots pictures of each of them. Both are dressed in thin silk robes.

My shocked look asks the question so Jayne answers, " Doreen thinks we are both, " Living Goddesses ", so we should take turns being the " Goddess " while the other girl, acts as the servant. I think it is fair since we are both beautiful, strong, shapely women that men fall over themselves to just talk to us. " That is when I finally realize that I am going home alone later if at all. This place is so different than any other home. Doreen suggested I sit and watch. She handed me a drink that tasted smooth and fruity. I needed it after this day. I just took a sip and watched the three of them laughing together. This is a place where angels dwell, bullies are banished and happiness comes first.

My eyes start to close as I fight it. I am suddenly tired and want to lay down. I hear Doreen saying " I will take care of you my dear friend. Here, let me get you to a bed in the little room ". I feel like I drank all day as she helps me onto the bed. I collapse onto my stomach unable to move anymore. I ask " Are my friends okay here tonight ? " Doreen answers in a low voice " Yes, they are, my friend. You are very tense and I will massage your shoulders and back. My hands will put you to sleep with sweet dreams " I want to pass out and start to let myself go. I feel her hands rubbing my shoulder and soothing my back as I smile and enjoy her warm touch. She is gentle and does have power in them. I then feel her hands under my blouse on my back as she unhooks my bra and says " You will be more comfortable. Let me undress you for a long sleep in my bed. Now I can see you up close and watch you sleep."

That was the last I could recall. When I awoke it was six in the morning and I was alone and naked in the bed. This room had pictures of Doreen everywhere and must have been her childhood room. My things were neatly folded with my bra and underwear on top. I quietly got dressed and decided to go home Those girls are all adults and I hope they are happy. I do not remember anything during the night but I have dreams about cookies, horses, a ten foot tall man and what looked like Sandra in that punchbowl. It was much bigger or she was smaller but in a dream all is not what it seems .I feel happy either way. I suddenly remember the drink and the fact that Doreen had scooped it out of the bottom of the punch bowl.

I walked out the front door but noticed the sign inside, on the hallway wall and what was written on it " Today - Book reading by Sandra will be Green Eggs and Ham ". Below that it said "

BREAKFAST - GREEN EGGS AND HAM " I stopped for a moment to read the ingredients, Scallion greens, farm fresh free range chicken eggs with honeybaked ham, optional - " If you are up, come down - If you are down, come up. fun will be had by all ". I turned to leave and knew Sandra would capture their ears, Janet had their taste buds tickled and Jayne had the palettes covered in oil paint, pencil, watercolors and pastels. Heavy on the gold and flesh colors. If I know her a new version of " The Birth of Venus ", starring Jayne, is the next masterpiece. We certainly did, steal the show.

All together now

That phone is ringing and ringing, should I let it go to the machine ? Yes, I will listen and screen it. Too early for much. " Hello, this Ray Vachon, a man that likes you. Maybe we could go for a ride in the country today if you are not busy ? You have my cell number. I am heading over to TED'S for breakfast. Beep ". This is a pleasant surprise and I must get up and get ready. I will have a coffee here with toast and let him enjoy his sausage and eggs with homefries and wheat toast. I know this because it is the other thing he orders besides the Daily Special. I asked him if he ever tries the eggs other ways ? " Oh no way. Jeanne asks me every time I order if I might try them scrambled, poached, sunny side up, hard boiled, over hard, eggs benedict ? " I shake my head side to side and then she reluctantly says " How about something different like over easy, Ray ? "

Again he answers BINGO. He is a funny, odd guy. I know he is smart and handsome. I have noticed other women turn to look at him. It must be his broad, square shoulders and clean cut look with a close shave. I smelled a hint of Old Spice on him and flashed back to my Dad. That must be a good thing I hope. Guys are very deceiving and learn how to trick a girl into their arms. The truth is I never looked at him when I ran over his foot but his words hit me first. I was expecting some rude guy to tell me to " Watch it or Where did you get your license, at Sears ? " No, he spoke in a clear voice saying he was okay and I should not worry. It was an accident. I felt worse than he did. I was put at ease by his words instantly. When he came around in front of me I saw a very attractive man. He dresses in a plain manner with a hat stating U.S. Army. Our few conversations have let me look into him alittle but today I am going to go for broke. I want to hear what he wants from me and life if he even thinks like that.

This will be hard to discuss with Ray but, in all fairness, I have to disclose my condition to him. My doctor, Miss Judie, has said there is no date written in stone when I may die but just her words hit me. It could happen tomorrow was a slim chance but chilling. She is always positive and I did insist she be up front and honest. The gypsy said I was very healthy but the outward signs are all she had to work with. My blood work and extra tests were not in her deck of cards that day. I liked it when Madame Betty said that " He will go away but not be far. This man has tough hands and a strong mind. I see him suffering and searching for his peace. Let the wind move him because he is not one to live a simple life .

Those words are a puzzle in my mind and I often wonder if he too has a secret about his future. I have to find out. My heart wants to love him and take him to my room each night. My life is fine but a strong man to carry me across this threshold would be nice. The loneliness catches me off guard and I feel low but really my fate is sealed. If I were to be fair to Ray I can not go any further than close friends. I want love and he may want it too but it feels different when we are older. Our eyes have seen time take its toll on people and death leaves one person alone and at a loss. Maybe this life being independent is something to be thankful for. So much to consider but for today I think we both deserve a day of fun and new memories like all of our little encounters has been, great.

" Hello Ray. This is Etta " and Ray replies " I just finished my breakfast, shall I pick you up ? In twenty minutes ? " I answer with a smile on my face " Yes Ray, pull up outside and beep ". I will go outside and sit on my steps to watch for him. He does not fool around and will be prompt.

My mind is wandering about what may happen today when I see his car pulling up so I stand up and walk to the curb. I wave to him as he pulls to a stop and then he toots his horn. Twice. He gets out and comes around to open my door as we give each other a hug. I smell that Old Spice again. Just then I hear Doreen open her window and call down to us " hey you two, down there, about to get into trouble doing things I can only imagine ? May I ask you both to visit for a few minutes or even a lifetime ? " I look at Ray and he is smiling. I shook my head to say yes and I realized that, this, will be our next big adventure together.

We walk to the gate and I press that thumb button and the gate opens wide. Ray speaks up " Quite interesting but it needs to be oiled. I can hear it squeak. That is not good because soon it will stop working correctly. I love to fix things." He takes my hand and we walk up the steps to the big front door. I do not see any visitors there today. Suddenly Doreen opens the door and hugs me while bowing slightly and then she asks " What is your name and do you follow orders ? " Ray just stands straight up and calmly says " Yes mam, I mean Miss, I am Ray and I like your big house. What else would you like to know ? " She motions for us to come in and we walk right through the house to the back yard where we all stop and sit.

Doreen turns to me and says with a straight face " I think this man needs to fill out an application for the First Mate of this ship. A man of the house who will live in the back of the carriage house. The suite, apartment, back there is very cozy and the view is fantastic if a guy likes looking at the woods and wildlife. There are many little things that need a handyman's touch. " Ray interjects " Like a squeaky front gate ? " Exactly sir, that and a million other jobs. The faucets leak, the boiler needs a tender and my horses need a guy to direct the girl groomers and stall helpers.

This place is a home for women of all ages and educations. If I like you and you need a new purpose in life, Ray,. this is a job and a home for you if you can stand to be surrounded by artists, musicians, chefs and a writer, as she looks directly at me.

If any lady takes a fancy to you she will have to visit your quarters including this gem next to you. Of course you know the way to her door ". Ray stood up and I thought he had enough but instead he said

" I like it very much. I like to have a list of things to do around a property. I can do any job you lay before me except for childbearing.

May I see these quarters you mentioned. I will know when I look at it. " He looks at me and I can see pain in his eyes but I feel wonderful. Maybe having him next door is enough for me to handle. My three best friends either live here or spend tons of time and tell me it is a paradise here of fun and learning.

There is never a dull moment inside these fences. Doreen leads us into the building thru the front, wide doors both now pushed open. we see the antique buggy there all ready to go and polished highly. It has written on the side " Captain Jones - Land Schooner ". Ray walks ahead of us to look into the stalls to see the horses. There are two young Spanish girls brushing them and they smile at us " Hola Patrona" as Doreen smiles at them.

Ray smiles at Doreen and says " Hello Boss " as they all laugh. I do not speak anything but good old English. Doreen is right though that a translator is needed here. Ray mentions the dozen languages he knows more or less.

Then I notice a large horse painting on the wall in front of us up high on the wall. I point and say " Who is that big fella Doreen ? " She replies " That is Rock, a great draft, pulling horse and a yearly champion at the Skowhegan Fair up in Maine for years. His blood is in these two here that pull me up a hill like I was in a four hundred horse powered car.

I bought this original piece from Pat Wooldridge, the acclaimed equine artist. She shows her works every year at the Fryeburg Fair where I commissioned this from her to grace my horses home. These horses love to look at their great-grand dads too.

That fair is where I first met Celia, the top pottery maker there. The truth with art and talent is that if you sell at that fair, you are real good at what you do. They run the top fair in New England and the country with the theme always " Country ". People travel there for oxen pulls, draft horse driving and cow milking in the Dairy Parlor for the public to view. I must get back there again."

The next two stalls are the smaller, thinner but muscular Arabian mares. Doreen moves to stroke their faces and I see their love for her. You can tell how a horse responds to a person as to how they are treated. Just like we do really but they are unable to fake it. A good swift kick speaks for them if unhappy and the ears go back.

Doreen opens a door that was hidden from us. It blended into the woodwork. I could see Ray smiling as he walked in. The little apartment was really four huge rooms. There is a woodstove in the living room. It has the looks that a man would call home. I could see Ray in here in his red L.L.Bean thermal union suit in heavy socks looking out at the falling snow. There were two bedrooms. One being the master room had a bathroom too. The thing I noticed was that he moved out onto the back porch and into the bright light of the sun shining down on him. The glass enclosure made it perfect for sunbathing from about noon until five every day. The view was just as Doreen had described. Woods as far as I could see and except for a new trail cut into the trees it looked untouched.

He turned to me and said to Doreen " I will accept your offer and move in right away. I have other things I do but you and all those here will be first. I was a soldier and will protect you all from evil. And you Etta may want to dump me now or we can go on being friends like we are now. I think you are great and this porch is my new piece of heaven.

My prayers have been answered. You know Etta that I feel like a heel dropping all this on you so suddenly. In this place I can lock the door, get a cold iced lemonade and get naked to sunbathe every day in peace. The sun has great healing powers ".

Now as he turns to me and moves closer I see that sign of him sweating again. This must have been very hard to say to us but it had to be done. I am in love with this whole place now too. Jayne, Sandra, Janet and Rania love it and will be here.

Maybe I will just shut up about my own fears and let him take the lead. We can still go out to do things and Doreen will be much better off with such a good guy watching over everything. Maybe her ship has come in finally. It is not in the Bay but she found it in Ray. Perhaps

I will continue on day to day like my doctor said to do. I might just surprise Ray with a glass of wine some cold, snowy night and enter his private quarters. I will only ask Doreen one thing. " Do not tell Ray about the " punchbowl night." Is That a deal Doreen ? " Absolutely she laughs out loud. My lips are sealed.

I will promise myself this for the rest of my life. It is good advice to run over the toes of every good looking man I meet but he must smell of Old Spice. They are the best.

Ray became the perfect man for Doreen and this renewed, living and breathing home. He had visited castles in Europe and loved this house, as much as those famous places around the world. There are many doors that are hidden in some of the rooms. The builder was a close friend of old Captain Jones and when the ship never returned, the men added secret, safety exits to protect her from thieves.

The widow was left with the few ships they owned to move spices from the Caribbean to Down East New England. There were some of his ships that were whaling vessels. It was considered to be, fishing, in colonial days.

The blubber from a whale could light the night in countless oil lamps. The brain had a finer oil used to lubricate the first machines of wood and metal. It was not a mean tradition back then. Those sailors were " iron men " on wooden ships.

Only the toughest and most daring of men would row out to a harpooned whale. That huge animal wanted to survive and easily turned to swallow more than one last morsel of man. The rumor in the village of Widow Port, about old skipper Jones, was that the biggest of all whales, Moby Dick, had taken them all to the bottom of the sea in the blink of an eye.

I know Auntie Carolina went up to the roof each day and often just read books or napped up there. Doreen has continued this practice but I would bet it was her bedtime, at dawn when she looked for the lost ship. There are some nights where everyone dips deeply into that punchbowl to live it up.

She has turned that stoic structure into a home for the lost, brilliant, gifted and ordinary, like me. Just the other day there was an open house to the whole village for them to see it up close. The cars came and went all day.

Well dressed ladies from high society were welcomed in to judge the many, many categories of life expressed here. Doreen was sure to include art, pottery, culinary masterpieces mixed with the living arts of music, visual wonders and rooms full dreams. The gardens themselves had a history of their own with one of a kind plants thriving in there.

This hedge from England, a section of tulips from Holland plus a cactus from Arizona on the shelves inside the greenhouse. The banquet that day was all paid for by Doreen. This was how she demonstrated to all that good came come from bad. It is said to follow your dream and she is, to the benefit of the world.

That night of the party I was able to be with my dear Ray again. We went into his suite, as it was now called. It was sweet too, he said. I noticed in just one week of meeting him that we changed our worlds. He is so happy now, it is on his face. He opened the door to the outside deck and took me by the hand out there.

We sat in the love seat swinging back and forth. The woods outback were dark but not silent. Crickets entertained our ears and once an owl hooted out for attention. It was very relaxing. Finally we are a couple of happy people. I do not worry anymore about my future. Yesterday I had a visitor next door at my place.

This very pretty, all business woman was at the door. " Hello Etta, I am Nancy, a realtor with Realty Vision down in the village. Doreen and I have been friends since childhood and she asked me to make you an offer to buy your little house for whatever you ask. You may live in it until you no longer want to or need to. Are you interested in that very kind offer ? "

I love Doreen and said " yes " immediately. Nancy hugged me and we both laughed. I will call my partner, Terry, to close the deal. Now the love nest can go back to the big house. Someday another couple can block the windows from peering eyes.

" Ray, tell me what the gypsy, Madame Betty said about me, please ? ". He smiled slightly and there were those beads of sweat forming on his brow so quickly. It must be haunting him ? Maybe I am not supposed to know. He then said simply " she will be the key to your happiness ", I did not understand then but now I do.

" You brought me to Doreen and this house. I am a twenty first century Renaissance man, living in a world of wonder within these gates. The crystal ball went black but then I saw these woods we look upon now. It must have been pointing to us sitting here together right now ? Now I can sunbathe in peace to heal my skin and at night, breath the pine scented, cool air.

My hands and fingers can now help the great people living here with any need they have. Then they can continue to express their talents. My specialty is fixing and protecting, two things I do best. Doreen has her guardian she needed and I do speak many words in any languages. It will help here in the new Widow Port. I will have the " daily special " for Ray now and then, plus we will go see Jeannie and the bumbleberry pie, together.

It just dawned on me, sitting here on this loveseat that I now have something to write about, us.

Beginning and end

Our relationship developed quickly as soon as I saw he had only interest in the house, helping others and just me. I moved into our love nest and now Doreen allows residents to couple up there with privacy.

It might be a spouse or whomever and if the sign is on the front door, " If the house is a rockin, don't come knocking ", we stay away. The story of the first newlyweds in there, on display, tickles many a bride now.

At first Ray and I were awkward in bed together although it was great and exciting. He liked to carry me over to the bed, treat me like a queen, feed me grapes and then go take a shower.

I could hurt him for that as I awoke from my daydream and raced into the shower with him. " Ray, do not start a fire if you do not have a hose ", I need to wash my mouth out with soap but I want what I want and I am tired of waiting.

He learned plenty about me that day and what a " hot " woman is capable of. We both had lovers in the past but I like a bright future and forget any bad past. It is possible to start again with someone, like a new car, just as powerful but a different body.

Ray is clean and shines in my eyes, our lovemaking is a two way street, with mutual communication and closeness. Neither of us are demanding and both feel satisfied about each day as we kiss goodnight.

The mornings always start with a light kiss and then we start our early morning moment. He likes a coffee with extra milk and one Equal with just toast, buttered. I have oatmeal, grapes and orange juice.

It is the most fun to just discuss yesterday and then what is to be done today. Both of us are growing in so many areas. These house residents are great thinkers and artisans plus Ray keeps it running smoothly.

There still is a " Punch Bowl " there but we stay back here in the Raven's nest, as Ray calls it. It seems he puts a dozen jumbo eggs on the deck and within ten minutes a big, black raven swoops down to take them. We both sat silently indoors and watched the giant bird rip the egg crate top off and then take an egg in the wide open beak.

Then it flies off for three minutes to cache it somewhere out in those thick woods. This is repeated twelve times until all are gone. One day an egg was stuck in the box so it punched the beak down into the egg and sucked it out.

I love nature and Ray does too so our feeders are full and suet hanging everywhere. In the spring, summer and fall the hummingbird feeders are kept full. I put them in the shade as the sun makes the red sugar water too hot to drink.

This collision of talents made us both smarter and yearning for more. How often can you be in a house of great knowledge and harmony ? Doreen has never been happier and is now a prominent lady about the village and on the world stage.

The guests here stay a week, a month or for unending periods. Most great minds must wander to see more, feel more. There is a big book at the door where each guest identified themselves and their first and last impressions. There have been no negative comments here.

One day Ray and I took the horses out onto the trails on a sunny day. He is at home with so many things including a full picnic basket to surprise me. It had the checkered tablecloth, wine with glasses and an assortment of containers filled by Janet, Sandra, Jayne and Rania with tender loving care.

Ray and I are considered the old couple in love, rolling in the hay, at the back of the barn. I am constantly asked simple questions, about love by the young girls, many from other lands and cultures.

This home is conservative in some ways to not offend others. Doreen insisted lovers use the Love Nest or " Go get a room somewhere ". That is fair in my opinion since sex and everything else are kept separate to be enjoyed uninterrupted.

I tell these girls that males in this country assume if you kiss with passion then you are ready for third base, skip second base, all the dating stuff. I only offer my humble opinion since I am divorced and considered a failure by many.

It might be that many couples are mismatched but stay together for a million reasons. I had one good reason and that was all I needed to move on. I can feel the true attention Ray gives to me and I try to never forget that as I give him a backrub or his favorite supper.

The second time around can be sweeter since both know things can be good or bad but it depends on what you both put into it. We hold hands walking in a store, I can not ask for much more. I like it when we can just sit and talk about things with no stress or drama like it was in my past.

He hates any fighting and usually is whistling while he works. I have met some of his other friends in person and on Skype. The old wrestler, Paul " the Butcher " Vachon, is related to him and that famous family. Then his cousins might call him to say hello, one a Harvard grad, others from Brown, all respect his well rounded life. Books do not make a person, by themselves without living things.

Recently I told Ray I had decided to write my first book and become a full, ranking member of the household, a great writer. I explained to him that it was a childhood dream but I never really felt moved to do it. My fears were like so many others must have " Do I have the talent, the ability ? I am no great thinker or wordsmith, no one will care what I say ".

It takes a confidence from deep within me to sit down to start but I want to as I am moved by love. This relationship is love, growing every day and both of us anxious to be alone each night. We are what we are, at this point in our lives, smarter and wiser than teenagers but just as eager.

When I started to tell Ray that I was going to write a book he was encouraging and positive. Then I asked him " May I tell about our great love story ? ". He smiled and said " Gee I feel kind of guilty because my dates may have bored you, right ? ".

I shook my head to say no and he continued with a bigger smile now " What about our showers, nude sunbathing, me dressed like a ballerina ? ". I laughed and said " You know you never did that and there is no outfit like that, big enough to fit a hunk like you ".

Please exaggerate on that part to make me The Man ". He need not worry because my story will be tame and decent like this romance is and will continue to be. He made me put " Love Potion Number Nine on the cd player and then Gypsy woman " as we laughed the night away. We like music to cuddle to and more. He makes me feel excited.

All the people in the big house encourage me because they say I am very aware of little things. I certainly feel inspired here surrounded by those born with talent or having achieved it. They are mostly very young but I can do it now, even though older.

I have Ray at my back to help me through it and and if I forget a word here and there he can catch it for me. My squeaky doors need oiling too and his opinion means plenty to me.

I will make him a nice big meal and he will politely listen as I read off the newest chapter I have completed. I do not want him to choke while eating if I see an interesting or funny part coming. The pace can be slowed down and maybe more with his dessert.

Back then as a kid I wanted to write fiction about a castle with the King and Queen, horses, in a place like Camelot. We all knew the song as enchanting as it told a story of every day being perfect. We all know good things come to an end but another love springs up somewhere else. The world goes round and round with children born every minute.

The human being feels cold, hot, hunger, pain and sorrow but strong love is the greatest thrill to lift someone. I am thankful I can feel things enough to notice it and now express myself in words. This will be fun and not an effort at all as my mind and heart spill it all out to the world. If anyone likes it I am now a real writer.

Page one, first sentence is as follows.

It was a casual encounter, in the aisle, at the grocery store ....

The end

About the author

He was raised in a blue collar family with two other brothers. Life was riding bicycles, baseball and being a Boy Scout. The Army needed him so he enlisted and served in Berlin at the Wall. Here a tour of duty at the Spandau Prison enabled him to see prisoner #7, Rudolf Hess, the last Nazi leader. The world opened up to him and now the stories of life fill his book.

Formerly a high tech computer expert, turned writer after an accident left him with a limp and " two left " feet, ending his dancing hobby. Now retired and writing for a year putting everything he has experienced in words of wisdom, knowledge and emotions. This attention to detail and being in unique situations allowed this book to be written.

Now living on a fixed income in a small town where an owl still calls during the night joined by the nearby whistle of a freight train blowing. The family consists of three sons, three grandchildren that call him " Grandfather " and keeping up with health issues as expected with age.

Dennis F. King

Clinton, Mass.

Front cover photo and picture of the author both taken on

Boylston Road in my town.

Proof

Made in the USA
Charleston, SC
08 December 2015